Praise for *Who Stole My Customer??*

"Everyone talks about becoming a customer-centered company. This practical and readable book shows how to actually make it happen."

— *Dr. Michael Hammer*
Author of the international bestseller Reengineering the Corporation

"*Who Stole My Customer??* offers unique and powerful insights into the world of acquiring and retaining customers. Most importantly it provides new approaches to keeping existing customers from defecting. A must-read in today's challenging business environment."

— *Dieter Huckenstein*
President, Hotel Operations, Hilton Hotels Corporation

"Harvey Thompson probably knows more than anyone else in the world about how companies should work with customers. In an age when computers and mass communications make it difficult to keep or attract new customers, Thompson's insights on what managers must do to keep them make this one of the most important business books published this year. Clearly a must-read for all levels of management."

— *James W. Cortada*
IBM Institute for Business Value

"Harvey Thompson has done it again with this well-written book that offers valuable insights about the roots of sustained corporate greatness. He captures a lifetime of building winning formulas and puts them into a simple and practical context for executives at any level looking to take their business to the next level in the 21st century."

— *Mark R. Richards*
President, Structures Division, Valmont Industries, Inc.

"One of the leading causes of the rapid turnover of marketing and sales executives isn't the economy, it's the ignored cancer of customer attrition. *Who Stole My Customer??* takes this challenge head-on and tackles it from a pragmatic perspective with actions you can take today."

— *Louis Columbus*
Senior Analyst, AMR Research

"I think Harvey Thompson really understands how customers feel about products and services—for better or worse! His central point is well taken: Take care of them now or lose them to competitors who are more in tune with your customers' needs and wants. This book helps us remember that we must build our offerings from the 'outside in' to build customer loyalty and minimize defection. Thank you, Mr. Thompson!"

— *Bill Ghormley*
Executive Consultant, The Forum Corporation,
and past President, The Marketing Science Institute

"With many customers focused on the 'next innovation,' Harvey Thompson straightforwardly breaks down the process for examining customer touchpoints and defection drivers and for recognizing and exploiting customer loyalty. Thompson also reaffirms the next value proposition in customer service: the customer's need for a solution. With that framework, he insightfully turns the magnifying glass 180 degrees to elicit the *reader's* experience as a customer. This helps drive home his message that a good part of success in customer acquisition and retention is dependent on continual reexamination of customer 'needs.'"

— *Michael Perry*
Chairman and Chief Executive Officer, IndyMac Bank

Who Stole My Customer??

Winning Strategies for Creating and Sustaining Customer Loyalty

Harvey Thompson

PRENTICE HALL
An Imprint of PEARSON EDUCATION
Upper Saddle River, NJ • New York • London • San Francisco • Toronto • Sydney
Tokyo • Singapore • Hong Kong • Cape Town • Madrid
Paris • Milan • Munich • Amsterdam

www.ft-ph.com

To my sons,
John and Josh.

Library of Congress Cataloging-in-Publication Data
Thompson, Harvey.
  Who stole my customer? : winning strategies for creating and sustaining customer loyalty
/ Harvey Thompson.
    p. cm.
  Includes index.
  ISBN 0-13-145356-4
    1. Customer loyalty. 2. Customer relations. 3. Customer satisfaction. I. Title.

  HF5415.525.T49 2003
  658.8'343--dc22

                                                    2003066028

Vice President, Executive Editor: *Tim Moore*
Editorial/Production Supervision: *Vanessa Moore*
Manufacturing Manager: *Alexis R. Heydt-Long*
Manufacturing Buyer: *Maura Zaldivar*
Interior Design: *Gail Cocker-Bogusz*
Cover Design Director: *Jerry Votta*
Cover Design: *Anthony Gemmellaro*
Editorial Assistant: *Rick Winkler*

© 2004 by Pearson Education, Inc.
Publishing as Prentice Hall
Upper Saddle River, New Jersey 07458

**Prentice Hall offers excellent discounts on this book when ordered in quantity for bulk
purchases or special sales. For more information, please contact: U.S. Corporate and
Government Sales, 1-800-382-3419, corpsales@pearsontechgroup.com.
For sales outside of the U.S., please contact: International Sales, 1-317-581-3793,
international@pearsontechgroup.com.**

Company and product names mentioned herein are the trademarks or
registered trademarks of their respective owners.

Printed in the United States of America
3rd Printing

ISBN 0-13-145356-4

Pearson Education Ltd.
Pearson Education Australia Pty., Limited
Pearson Education Singapore, Pte. Ltd.
Pearson Education North Asia Ltd.
Pearson Education Canada, Ltd.
Pearson Educación de Mexico, S.A. de C.V.
Pearson Education—Japan
Pearson Education Malaysia, Pte. Ltd.

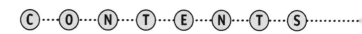

CONTENTS

The purpose of this book is to introduce powerful new approaches to help you keep your customers. Managing customer retention and loyalty is now the top issue for CEOs globally (see Figure 3.2 on page 24). The book expands and builds upon concepts introduced in *The Customer-Centered Enterprise* (McGraw-Hill, 2000), which predicted the global shift in business strategy from product to service and the current upward spiral in customer attrition. Key concepts, such as *take the customer viewpoint,* are further developed to generate critical customer loyalty and stem the tide of customer defection.

To help you get and then adopt the customer's perspective, the issues are presented from both a company viewpoint as well as that of a customer—because both views must be reconciled and aligned. Each chapter concludes with a *You Are the Customer* exercise, i.e., you turn your management hat around and personally experience the loyalty or attrition issues from an actual customer's perspective and then consider what must change within your firm.

The book shares what has been learned from customer-centered research, development, and innovation to build world-class customer-focused (and customer-preferred) organizations around the world, including the massive IBM global transformation. You may not require the same level of detail as other readers with different organizational roles; however, you will share a common need for practical, actionable information to stimulate thinking and enable your decision-making. A real effort has been made to keep this book at such a level—potentially valuable to all—and not a textbook of task-level minutiae.

When their customers leave, managers and business owners want to know: **Who stole my customer??** How? What can we do to keep customers and attract new ones? How can we become customer centric and customer preferred? What are the alternatives to temporarily buying customers with points or discounts from so-called (and easy to copy) "loyalty cards"? What is new, world-class, leading-edge thinking on the topic? Where is the greatest leverage to improve our business? Which customer-oriented investments offer the best return? What are the typical elements and major issues involved? What are the possible benefits? What are the impacts of not doing it? What pitfalls and exposures are already known by those who have a customer-centric business strategy?

I'll share some answers with you as if you are a client who is considering investing in a world-class customer strategy to expand and *keep* your market share. This book is intended to inform and interest you to go to the next steps, i.e., move far beyond "Have a nice day" platitudes and develop a customer-defined, outside-in vision of your business, plus the capabilities and infrastructure to make it a reality

Then let your competitors ask, **Who stole their customers??**

I wish you good reading.

— Harvey Thompson
Your Executive Consultant and Customer Advocate

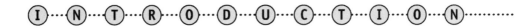

You are a customer.

You are considering your next purchase—perhaps to replace an old, well-used product, or possibly to buy a new item or service that you have never before owned.

Think about it. What will drive your decision regarding where you will conduct this business? What determines whether you do business with one provider of a product versus another? And later, will you return and purchase again from that firm or move on to a new source?

In today's environment, one firm's products pretty much resemble those of other potential vendors. When a company does introduce a truly unique product idea, their innovation is soon replicated and available from virtually everyone else in their industry. Improvements to existing product lines are also quickly copied by competitors. So, considering the similarities, the product itself is often not the reason that you select one provider over another.

Consider how you make your buying decisions and how you determine where to conduct your business. Is it strictly based on the product, or do other factors come into play? For example, if you are already a customer and familiar with a firm's products and services, to what extent can the *touchpoint* experiences you have had (i.e., *shop, buy, pay, delivery,* and *post-sale service)* influence whether you will return to purchase there again or defect and buy elsewhere?

If you learned that a firm, with which you have had no experience, provides great benefit and value during such customer interactions, might you drive across town to purchase from them, although similar products are available nearby? Do you already do that today? Is your favorite source for clothes the nearest haberdashery, or do you travel past nearby stores and shopping areas to get to a preferred retailer? Is your current bank the one most conveniently located to you? Is your car serviced at the closest professional mechanic or gas station, or at the absolutely lowest-cost provider? If not, then why not? Why do you drive past one potential provider to get to another?

In the past, consumers had to walk or drive to obtain most products and services. Still, they often did not select providers simply on the basis of proximity or a prior relationship. Today, location or a prior business relationship can have even less importance in their selection of a vendor. With overnight or express delivery service, one can literally conduct a global search for the best possible source via the Internet, and often can switch their customer account to a new provider with a mouse-click. So, if you are like most consumers, the *customer experiences* during touchpoint interactions are increasing as the motivators to remain a customer or to leave. Bad experiences during interactions with a current vendor can easily drive you away, even though you are satisfied with their products, because alternative sources are literally a click away. And extraordinary, positive experiences during touchpoint interactions can give you an incentive to stay with a vendor—or if offered elsewhere, could also attract or **steal you away**.

Question: What if such powerful touchpoint interactions were actually designed by you to provide the things you most value during those moments? What if a vendor identified you as a highly desired customer (perhaps based on your financial, psychological, or other characteristics) and let *you* design *their* business to provide the greatest possible value to you? What if—even though their products and prices were similar to others—your interactions with them during your *shop, buy, pay, receive,* and *post-sale service interactions* were completely designed into their business, outside-in, and from YOUR perspective?

Can you envision being attracted away from your current bank, automobile dealer, airline, hotel chain, financial services firm, insurance company, retail store, or so on because someone with a relatively equal product knew you, valued you, and did things *your* way? Can you envision how you could receive value that would differentiate a firm if their sales processes were designed to make your own purchase process fast, easy, and low cost? Could a firm's knowledge of you and your long-running relationship with them enable a more personal, high-value, consultative sales or service relationship that would make them your preferred provider?

For example, if a car dealership, or financial services firm, or audio/video store had a selling process that was literally defined by you to ideally meet your needs, and given that their products were equal or similar to others', would you move your business there? Can you envision how you could later receive extraordinary benefit during interactions with their service processes, if those were also designed from your perspective to make it easy, quick, and ideally convenient for you?

What if that company's invoicing or billing statements were also designed from your viewpoint, to make it easy to reconcile, pay them, and keep your records, might you prefer doing business with them over others? How about a telephone company bill that you could readily understand, have confidence in, and conveniently pay? If their products were similar, would such a process or service win your business?

If you are like the hundreds of customers with whom I have met and facilitated in creative, business *visioneering* exercises, then your answer to each of the above is, "Yes."

So, if you already know the above to be true when *you* are a customer, why isn't *your* business already doing that with *your* own customers? You are likely both a customer and a provider of goods and services! That's true of most managers, but somehow, when they change hats and assume their provider or vendor roles, managers lose sight of the customer perspective. Instead of designing and measuring business processes and customer touch-points from their customers' viewpoints (outside-in), managers shed their customer skins, don their management hats and adopt the perspective of the firm (inside-out). Touchpoint interactions and supporting infrastructure are designed from the company's point of view to optimize internal processes, based on an under-standing of what may have minimally satisfied customers in the *past*—possibly back when the firm was more successful. Ironically, when in the role of customers, a firm that allowed them to define and design high-value touchpoint interactions would attract those same managers, however they do not do that with their own customers and are losing them at an accelerating rate. Sound familiar? It should, because it occurs in all industries and is a major obstacle for even the most well-intentioned management teams.

We will use several techniques in subsequent chapters to overcome this "inside-out" business orientation and help you to more effectively fulfill your role as a business leader. It will not be enough to simply cite to you innovative new ways to become customer centric and retain loyal customers. You have already read business books and articles on such topics, but always with your inside-out filters on. We must overcome the company-first viewpoint that has been ingrained into you from the time you attended your first business course, management seminar, or company meeting. You have been programmed with certain common, business-driven approaches to develop your mission, vision, strategies, plans, and programs. The problem is that those always only include the customer—as opposed to being actually developed, designed, and driven by them. And when you do read a book that promotes how to take more of an outside-in customer viewpoint, you read that material while mentally and emotionally still wearing your company hat. You do not move past mere intellectualization of the material, or viscerally experience the truth of it so it becomes a part of your actual system of beliefs.

To truly understand and appreciate such customer-centric materials, you must take off your current industry or company management hat and consider the concepts from fresh perspectives. In the effort to contrast a company viewpoint versus a customer viewpoint, the examples used in this book will often be automobile companies or banks because *you* are a customer of those, and you will be able to visualize and internalize how to improve them from an actual *customer's point of view*. The customer-centered concepts we will cover are generic and do not apply to only one industry, so once you consider and internalize them via a bank or automotive example, you can later apply them to your own industry and firm.

For instance: within the examples we will examine the points of view of executives in those firms, so that you can see how *they* see *you* as a customer. Then we will place you into the role of the customer, so you can shed your management hat (and the inside-out business viewpoint that accompanies it) as you consider the innovative customer-centric approaches being discussed.

We begin, in Part 1, with an introduction to an automobile company and the case for action to become more customer centric, attract, and keep your customers.

1

Customer Defection: The Case for Action

"We have met the enemy, and he is us."

— Walt Kelly, in POGO

1

When Prior Strengths Become Your Weaknesses

R ecently, I stood in a boardroom and spoke with the top-tier executives of a major automobile manufacturer famous for its brand and renown for engineering and product excellence.[1] The brand had enjoyed a loyal following for decades, but it was now losing market share, and in the U.S. customer defection was nearly 70 percent. In other words, for every ten U.S. customers who bought their cars, approximately

---

1. Not the European auto company discussed in: Thompson, Harvey. *The Customer-Centered Enterprise: How IBM and Other World-Class Companies Achieve Extraordinary Results By Putting Customers First.* McGraw-Hill, 2000.

seven would defect—only three would return to buy again. To understand this trend, my consulting team had conducted extensive interviews at their headquarters, as well as workshops with dealers (their distribution channel), and focus groups with their customers and former customers. It was time for our mid-engagement client review.

We knew what the problem was. Their customers had told us. Now, I had a problem of my own: how to tell the auto executives that *they* were the problem.

They had become their own worst enemy. Their strength and prior success as a product-focused firm had now become their greatest weakness and exposure. The world had changed and they had not. Often with great success comes at least two negative results: arrogance and inertia. When a marketplace changes, as it ultimately will, arrogance and inertia can prevent a successful organization of good managers from being able to sense those changes and respond by also changing. The very attributes that once contributed to the company's rise to greatness, such as pride in their own product and service knowledge, can subsequently doom them to wither and fail, by not listening to their (less knowledgeable, non-expert) customers.

I began my executive presentation with a story about another major corporation, the IBM company, and I described IBM's similar experiences with great success followed by customer defection and failure. Throughout the 1960s, '70s, and '80s, IBM enjoyed remarkable growth based upon product excellence and, arguably, the world's greatest marketing and sales team of the era. IBM leveraged its enormous research and development capabilities to invent new products and technological advances, and then instructed its customers on why the products were needed and how to use them. IBM then serviced and maintained those leading-edge products for their less skilled customers.

Few companies during that period had the infrastructure, knowledge, or capabilities to analyze their own data processing needs, or to install, operate, and service the complex IBM offerings. So, customers became increasingly dependent upon "Big Blue" with each round of IBM product innovation. IBM's core competencies were to develop and then push new products out to a dependent, if not passive, and trusting marketplace.

However, by the 1990s, competition increased with the entry of new vendors who introduced competencies that included an ability to listen to customers and then give them what they wanted. While these new entrants focused on the customer, listened, and rapidly responded with offerings, IBM continued its internal, expert-driven focus on product and service development. Arrogance and inertia, bred from years of prior success, prevented deviating from the established IBM processes that had yielded positive results for decades. IBM continued to rely on historic functional and competitive strengths of research and development, manufacturing, and marketing that were designed to invent new things and then sell them—not to listen and then flexibly respond. As a result when the market changed in the early '90s, IBM missed that transition. Customers had developed their own internal support staffs, and many were no longer dependent on a vendor to tell them what they needed or how to use it. Further, this new generation of customers had developed strong opinions and demanded more user-friendly and *customer-defined* products and services. Customers, for example, had come to expect that hardware and applications work the way that they worked—not the other way around. By the mid-90s, IBM market share plunged and stock prices fell from $110 to $37 per share. IBM's historic strengths and internal self-reliance as *the expert* had literally become their Achilles' heel and almost ruined the company.

I concluded the analogy and told the auto executives the good news was that we had learned from our mistakes and—as a matter of survival—IBM had now made an art and science of how to listen to customers and develop business capabilities to provide what they want. We were there to share with the client's management team what we had recently learned from *their* automotive customers, so they would not repeat IBM's mistakes of the early 1990s. It was intended to be a way of saying to my client, "Don't be arrogant (like we were); listen to your customer."

The room was deathly quiet, and they looked at me as if I were speaking a language from another planet. Apparently the only point to which they agreed was regarding IBM's arrogance—particularly mine. During a quick break called by the CEO, a member of his staff confided to me that the culture in this firm was that they had little to learn from outsiders, and they particularly did not trust or listen to consultants. Further, they knew their own business better than anyone; that's why they had been so successful all those years.

Chapter 1
When Prior Strengths Become Your Weaknesses

Hmmm, the first deadly sin of a successful firm: *arrogance,* as the experts. As well as the second sin: *resistance to change.*

Our meeting resumed, and over the next hour I learned that the comment about the firm not listening also applied to their customers. They had little regard for direct customer feedback when it conflicted with their own views or prior customer experiences. When we cited desires, issues, or concerns raised by their customers, the executives often countered with their own personal beliefs and discredited or belittled what their customers had said. As an example, when told that in their deteriorating U.S. marketplace American consumers visiting an automobile showroom tend to immediately examine a car's coffee-cup holders, a top European auto exec retorted, "We build cars for driving, not for drinking coffee." The correctness of his (internal) view was supported by vigorous head-nods around the board table. At that moment a chart could be seen on the wall behind me, from one of their industry's most respected consumer research firms, which screamed that seven out of ten of this firm's U.S. customers would not return.

Silly customers. We know best.

So, what was the problem? Who had **stolen their customers**? (And why did they leave?)

Pogo knew. *We have met the enemy and he is us.*

You Are the Customer

You are a customer.

What attracts you? What can move you later to change vendors?

Can you think of times when a company's strengths—and what made it attractive to you—were that it had the knowledge, skills, and experience that you did not? Can you remember feeling insecure or anxious because you lacked a critical set of knowledge, skills, or capabilities? Do you remember the value you placed on a relationship with someone who did have those skills and stepped in to fill the void?

It might have been because you lacked relatively common experience in some critical area and therefore had no knowledge or skills. Or it might have been because the topic was leading edge and newly introduced, and knowledge was actually uncommon and resident in limited clusters of specialists. Possibly it was simply due to a lack of headcount or staff on your part—or a shortage of both: people *and* skills.

Think about the relief and value propositions that such expert providers of products and services have brought to you when you were an inexperienced customer. Their successes enabled your success and the better they became as the experts, the more you benefited.

However, when you later developed your own expertise and self-reliance, did your needs change regarding how you subsequently acquired and used those products or services? Did the firms need to also change to retain your business?

As the market for such an item matures in the future and you become a more informed and capable consumer, would you want to give input to your providers and add your own needs, wants, and requirements to their design specs? How would you feel about a vendor who continued to play the role of *expert* and expected you to be a passive user/recipient?

Would you still highly value someone whose value proposition persisted to be that they would tell you what you need, or do it for you?

As your confidence to know your own needs evolves, how might your expectations and requirements for other touchpoint interactions also change? If such a supplier's approach remained unchanged, do you think you could be attracted away by a new vendor who would team with you and utilize *your* user expertise as input into the design of their products, services, and touchpoints? Could you be **stolen** away by such a value proposition?

- What about *your* customers? What were the strengths that originally made your firm a success in their eyes?
- How are you evolving your core competencies in order to stay aligned with a changing marketplace? How does your company listen to customers and make them the relentless

focal point for the design of products, services, and customer-facing processes? How does your company sense the changes in the marketplace and what your customers value, and then respond to those? How does your firm anticipate and prepare for those, in advance?

- When *you* are a customer, you know what moves you today to change vendors. What if you were *your* customer? Could you be easily **stolen** away? What if you were your competitor? What might you do to attract away customers? If you aren't doing those things today, who is the enemy responsible for your lost customers tomorrow?

2

A Boutique, Alternative Strategy of the 1990s

W hat is more difficult to manage than a struggling young company? The answer is often a previously successful old company—and the more success that a firm has enjoyed in the past, the harder it can be to maintain. The enemy at that automobile company was not bad managers, but rather bad *management practices*, which were once the accepted norms and remain well entrenched in established firms today.

The company merely reflected the mindset of its industry; automobile manufacturing has historically been a product-focused enterprise, and *product-focused* traditionally meant from an internal or company viewpoint. Until recently this was true of most manufacturing endeavors and not just automobile companies. With the exception of automation and robotics for economies of scale, most of the significant, post-industrial-revolution changes in manufacturing were driven by the quality-mania of the 1980s and 1990s—not by a focus on customers.

MANUFACTURING: *MOTHER OF ALL* PRODUCT-FOCUSED STRATEGIES

The international focus on product quality was initiated by Japanese firms in the 1950s, ironically ones with a global image for cheap, low-quality products (such as dime store toys made of tin). To rebuild Japan's post-war manufacturing capabilities and become more competitive, the Union of Japanese Scientists and Engineers (JUSE) brought Dr. W. Edwards Deming from the U.S. to Japan, where his statistical quality control methods became the basis for the JUSE (now globally respected) Deming Prize for quality. These product disciplines were wholeheartedly embraced and adopted by Japanese management, cross-industry, and by the 1980s, the impacts were felt worldwide. Japanese competitors with high-quality products literally forced a subsequent, global crusade for *quality*. In the U.S., for example, the marketplace for automobiles was shifted (no pun intended) from a bias toward *Made In America* to a demand for *Made With Quality*. As American auto companies struggled to find new methods to compete with the higher-quality products of Toyota and Honda, the quality issue relentlessly spread to other industries.

MANUFACTURING: *MOTHER OF ALL* PRODUCT-FOCUSED STRATEGIES (continued)

Ultimately, high-tech Motorola developed its methodical "Six Sigma" program to deliver a .999997 level of quality to manufacturing processes. Designed initially for the manufacturing of electronic products, such as cell phones, the Motorola Six Sigma methods also provided a leading-edge means to improve the performance of many other processes. The approaches and their world-class results were considered a high-performance-attainment model (benchmark) for those who aspired to compete on the basis of extraordinary quality. In that era, business strategy and how firms chose to compete (e.g., their value proposition to attract market share) were focused almost universally on product not customer, and certainly not on customer service.

During the 1990s, a few notable firms began to emerge—primarily in the service sectors, such as financial services—that based their strategic differentiation (e.g., how they would make their firm uniquely attractive to customers) on being customer-centered and by identifying and then delivering customer needs during service or touchpoint interactions. Firms such as MBNA America Bank (a credit-card bank) staked out a strong competitive position on customer service and a reputation for being customer-centric; i.e., customers—and fulfilling customers' needs —are the major design points for their business. A focus on the customer, and on service as a differentiator, was so seldom seen at the time that many such companies became infamous as customer zealot icons.

Although some firms notorious for service and customer-focused strategies became incredibly successful in the 1990s (see Figure 2.1), their product-focused counterparts viewed customer-focused strategies as mere anomalies to be employed by the few. Being customer-centric was considered an alternative (as in *alternative lifestyle*) or boutique business strategy. Being a product-centric company and relying on a firm's internal experience, knowledge, and capabilities continued to be the primary basis for mainstream business strategy in the '90s.

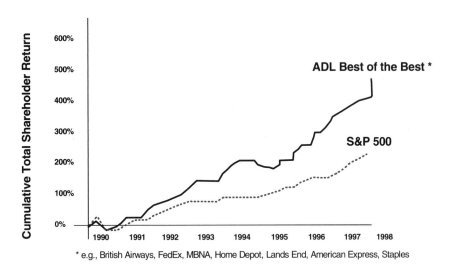

* e.g., British Airways, FedEx, MBNA, Home Depot, Lands End, American Express, Staples

Figure 2.1 1990s—The secret: "Boutique Strategy" outperforms S&P 500. Source: Adapted from a report by AD Little.

Chapter 2
A Boutique, Alternative Strategy of the 1990s

The S&P 500 was the performance standard by which share-holder value and growth were measured in the '90s. Ironically, while these companies enjoyed huge market success and notoriety, a study late in the decade revealed a parallel phenomenon: a group of firms, more notable for being customer-centric, had greatly outperformed the product-focused S&P 500. This information did little to sway the common view that internal-driven and product-focused strategy would continue as "the right way." It would not be until the start of a new millennium that this would change and the *alternative*, boutique strategy of the '90s would become a strategic *imperative* and a matter of survival for the 2000s.

You Are the Customer

What about when you are the customer?

Can you think of how your own viewpoint has changed over the past few years, based on what was available in the marketplace? Think of the companies you most admired 15 or 20 years ago. Who were they?

Were they the famous manufacturing brands, renowned for their products, such as GE, IBM, or General Motors? Were they the quality-movement-pioneer Japanese automobile firms, such as Toyota? Or the Six Sigma American manufacturer Motorola? How many non-manufacturing (or non-product-focused) firms can you think of that were considered "most admired" from that era?

Now, think about a decade ago—the early '90s. Can you name a company that was famous for customer service, or customer centricity, and not its product? If so, was that firm typical of the business world? Or, was it an anomaly and icon for an uncommon, customer-focused culture, such as Nordstroms or L.L. Bean? Within the entire Fortune 500, or the S&P 500, how many firms can you name that were famous and appealed to *you* as their customer by being truly customer centric? Two out of 500? Five out of 500? How many more?

What about as recently as five to seven years ago? What companies come to your mind as having the greatest reputations and
mind-share as brands in the global marketplace? Were they high-
tech manufacturing and product houses, such as Microsoft and
Intel? Others? How many came to mind that were non-product
oriented?

So, how did you feel as a customer, when you first actually heard
of, or had a truly exceptional, customer-focused experience in the
early '90s? Were you surprised, excited, or delighted?

How has that changed for you today? Is an excellent customer
experience still as unexpected and delightful as it was in 1994? Or
do you now tend to expect such treatment?

- What about *your* customers? How did you treat your
  customers in the 1990s? Was your firm a practitioner of a
  product-centric strategy that strived to match the
  performance of the S&P 500? Or were you a pioneer of the
  emerging, boutique customer-focused strategies? What
  about today?

- Your own expectations change greatly when you are the
  customer. Have *your customers'* expectations also changed
  since the 1990s? How has your treatment of them changed?

3

A Survival Issue and Strategic Imperative of the 2000s

Today, as the automotive company mentioned earlier has learned, is a new day. What worked in the old environment, such as competing based on the attributes of your products, no longer works. Technology has rendered most new products easy to copy, with shorter lead times for competitors to ramp up production of their own version. Improvements to differentiate existing products—such as true advancements in a soap product to get clothes "whiter than white" or the addition of slide-out room expanders to make an SUV a "home away from home"—often provide little time to enjoy industry leadership or to recoup the investment. As a result, firms must now look for new forms of customer-focused value delivery to supplement their fundamentally undifferentiated products.

Some examples: How truly different is a Toyota from a Nissan? How dissimilar are Vanguard's financial products from those of American Express? Are United Airlines' planes and seats really that different from American Airlines'? Are vehicles provided by Avis truly unique when compared to those from Hertz? If blindfolded, can you tell the difference between your hotel room at a Sheraton versus a Hilton? Without the logo, can you recognize an RCA television sitting next to a Sanyo? No? Then how are these firms to attract your business in the future, much less motivate you to be their loyal customer who returns time and again?

Price, you say? Differentiate by having a lower price? Or perhaps offer discounts or airline points to your frequent customers via a so-called "loyalty card"? Today both of these are common, easily matched, and tend to increase the customers' view of your offerings as commodities—as multiple-loyalty-card holders tend to jump from vendor to vendor for the best (price or points) deal. More and more, low prices and/or loyalty card benefits are merely a means to stay in the game—not to win it.

In most industries, companies must now look for a new basis to differentiate and compete. What they find is that successful boutique strategy firms of the '90s had the answer: Focus on the customer, not the product, for a unique customer value proposition. Business strategy has become *customer strategy* in order to stay in business, and customer centricity is now imperative and no longer the optional or alternative strategy that it once was. Customer-management and customer-facing business processes (and the *customers' experience and value received* during interactions with those processes) are now the most critical levers for business success (see Figure 3.1).

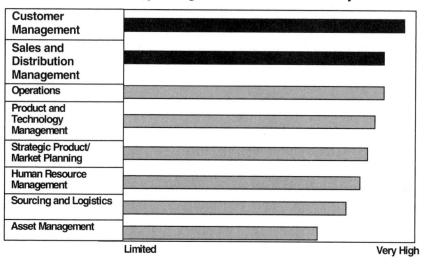

"Which processes, if improved, would you expect to yield the greatest potential benefits for your organization in the next 3 to 5 years?"

	Limited Very High
Customer Management	
Sales and Distribution Management	
Operations	
Product and Technology Management	
Strategic Product/ Market Planning	
Human Resource Management	
Sourcing and Logistics	
Asset Management	

Figure 3.1 2000s—The shift from product to customer and customer-facing processes. Source: Adapted from a survey by AD Little.

With the movement in strategy from product to customer (and to the value customers can receive during touchpoint interactions), firms in most industries are now working to engineer a *winning customer experience*. This has generated an upward spiral in the level of service and customer-friendly products being enjoyed by their most valued customers (often elsewhere and with other industries). New technologies such as the Internet, enterprise-wide databases, data mining, and mass-customization-capable processes have turbo-charged the level of tailoring and personalization that is now possible. E-business transactions on consumers' personal Web sites at a Fidelity.com or a Schwab.com can be tailored to the tastes, interests, and needs of the individual customer. After all, with the electronic delivery of products, services, or information, there is often little incremental cost to arrange those electrons the way the customer wants on his or her personal screen.

However, with each excellent, personalized service experience, customer expectations are also reset upward and that level becomes the base *expectation* the next time. This rising level of expectations spills over to subsequent interactions with other firms. A great experience at Amazon.com, such as a personalized offering that anticipates your needs, becomes an expectation the next day when dealing with the cable TV company. A delightful interaction with Company A becomes that customer's expectation when dealing later with Company B. A great experience in one industry also raises expectations in dealing with other industries, even though cost structures and levels of technology may vary widely between those industries. If, for example, Audi and Infiniti provide a loaner car while a vehicle is being repaired, their customers may then anticipate the same treatment from Dell Computer. Customers are being conditioned to expect ever-higher levels of service and will be unhappy if it isn't provided. And they will move themselves (e.g., defect or **steal away**) to get it.

Further, new expectations can be set by one customer-friendly channel (such as the Internet), where it is uniquely cost-efficient and cost-effective, and then become an expectation during subsequent interactions with all channels. As a result, companies in virtually all industries are now scrambling to stay up with rising customer demands for increased levels of product and service usability and personalization.

During the 1990s, this occurred at a relatively slow pace set by a few innovator-practitioners of boutique, customer-focused approaches to business strategy. Today, however, firms in most industries are quickly being dragged into the fray, and to this mode of competition, by their customers. Why? Because the Internet provides much more than business capabilities to personalize service; it also provides *one-click ease of defection* to the customers. Consumers can now leisurely search the planet for the best match to their needs, and with a mouse-click open a new account with a new provider in, say, Ireland or India—wherever and whenever they choose. As a result, one of the greatest business issues today is *customer retention*. The book *The Customer-Centered Enterprise*[1] covered the initial strategic move from product to customer. Now a second, powerful movement has also resulted: the shift from customer relationship and satisfaction management to customer loyalty and attrition management.

The consensus top management issues and critical levers of business success for CEOs have recently changed for the first time

---

1. Thompson, Harvey. *The Customer-Centered Enterprise: How IBM and Other World-Class Companies Achieve Extraordinary Results By Putting Customers First.* McGraw-Hill, 2000.

in a century. Although new management tools have often been introduced, the fundamental top priorities for businesses have remained constant for decades:

- Increase revenue

- Reduce costs

- Improve profitability

However, the early 2000s have already seen customer defections increase with such force that customer loyalty and retention have literally become the top CEO issues (see Figure 3.2).

Top CEO Management Issues

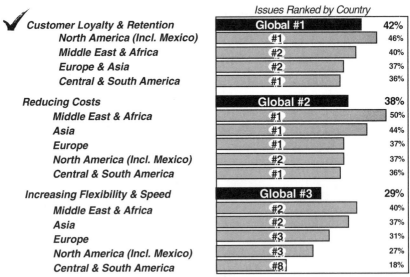

	Issues Ranked by Country	
✓ **Customer Loyalty & Retention**	Global #1	42%
North America (Incl. Mexico)	#1	46%
Middle East & Africa	#2	40%
Europe & Asia	#2	37%
Central & South America	#1	36%
Reducing Costs	Global #2	38%
Middle East & Africa	#1	50%
Asia	#1	44%
Europe	#1	37%
North America (Incl. Mexico)	#2	37%
Central & South America	#1	36%
Increasing Flexibility & Speed	Global #3	29%
Middle East & Africa	#2	40%
Asia	#2	37%
Europe	#3	31%
North America (Incl. Mexico)	#3	27%
Central & South America	#8	18%

Figure 3.2 What are your top management issues? Source: "The CEO Challenge," a survey by The Conference Board of nearly 700 global business leaders.

Chapter 3
A Survival Issue and Strategic Imperative of the 2000s

Creative management tools are once again required, and critical new customer retention (not acquisition) capabilities are now necessary. Only a few short years ago, it was difficult to engage senior executives to discuss customer service, customer centricity, customer loyalty, and attrition management as a focus for business strategy and investments. The Conference Board survey reflects how this has changed and the dramatic elevation in importance that CEOs now place on customers and customer service worldwide.

Why? Because they have to.

Why? Because customers now require it.

Why? Because others now provide it, and to survive so must they all or their customers will leave.

Based on the sponsorship I receive to speak to executive teams, the chart in Figure 3.2 has become quite real to me. Not long ago, the host was typically an executive responsible for a single, customer-facing function or process, such as sales or service. Today, such briefings are rapidly increasing and are sponsored by the chief executive or a senior, enterprise-level leader, and the scope has grown from a functional- or process-specific topic to a more strategic and enterprise-wide discussion. The purpose is typically to help senior executives convey to their teams the urgency of becoming customer centric as well as to introduce leading-edge, practical approaches.

Why now? Because the customer and his or her loyalty has risen to #1 on the CEOs' radar screens as a major business issue!

This remarkable change of priorities has done more than elevate customer relationships and customer management into a new, strategic light: The actions that comprise customer management have also been reprioritized. Rising attrition, caused by the rapid increase in service quality by competitors and easy, Internet-enabled, one-click defection, has literally reversed the priorities for customer relationship management or CRM (see Figure 3.3):

· From **attract**, develop, and then retain customers
· To **retain** customers, then attract new ones, and develop both

Customer management, or customer relationship management, has historically been viewed as a continuum, i.e., acquire, develop, and retain. Business priorities (and investments) have almost always been in that order, with the emphasis on *acquire*. For example, entire functional organizations and processes such as sales and marketing are devoted to customer acquisition. But how often have you heard of a Senior Vice President of Customer Development? Or an Executive Vice President of Customer Retention? Sales and marketing have traditionally been considered the primary levers for basic business survival, much less for growth. Today, however, that must change (see Figure 3.3).

There have always been profit leverage and incentives to *retain* and sell to current customers, rather than incur high cost of sales to attract and sell to new ones, but this groundswell movement of customer retention to a strategic focus is more recent. In the

Greatest Challenges in Customer Management

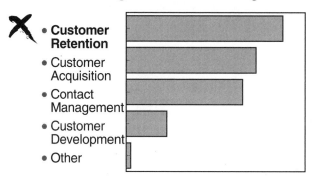

Figure 3.3 2000s—The shift to customer retention (loyalty) as a strategic imperative. Source: ADL survey of more than 130 major U.S. corporations.

current environment, *competitors attract your customers away* through extraordinary levels of personalized products and service, so you must work harder to both retain your old customers as well as acquire new ones. And, given the financial leverage if you sell to existing customers (potentially nine times more profit versus acquiring new ones), the retention of existing customers is now one of the highest priorities in business.

One study[2] has demonstrated that, depending on the industry, a reduction in the percentage of customer defections of 5 to 10 percent can yield up to 75 percent in additional profit. The study

---

2. Conducted by the Wharton School and published in the *Harvard Business Review* (also cited in: Thompson, Harvey. *The Customer-Centered Enterprise: How IBM and Other World-Class Companies Achieve Extraordinary Results By Putting Customers First.* McGraw-Hill, 2000.).

documented that, due to the lower cost of sales, there is huge financial benefit and profit growth if you simply retain your existing customers, without any additional growth in sales volume.

The impact of a 70 percent defection rate on the automobile firm provides a good example of this, especially when the firm's relative competitive position is examined—as depicted in Figures 3.4 through 3.7.

Customers Who Repurchase
(Loyalty Rates)

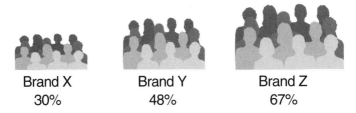

Brand X	Brand Y	Brand Z
30%	48%	67%

Figure 3.4 Customer loyalty experienced by Brand X. Example adapted from industry customer loyalty data.

Loyalty, in this example, is the reciprocal, or opposite, of a brand's defection rate. When only 30 percent of the automotive firm's customers are loyal and return to buy a car again, then 70 percent of them do not return but defect to a competitive product. (Other definitions of loyalty can include factors such as whether customers also return for parts or service, but such factors are not in this example.)

The automotive market does not expand at a rate sufficient for all the firms to attain their annual growth objectives by simply maintaining their current share. For any one company (see Figure 3.4) to grow significantly, it must capture (**steal**) customers or market share from the other competitors; this is known in the auto industry as *conquest*. Conquest is expensive, since it costs much more to market to, attract, and then sell to new customers than to merely fulfill the orders of returning ones. As a result, there is a major impact on the profitability and shareholder value for Brand X versus its competitors, due to the costs associated with Brand X's greater need for conquest (see Figures 3.5 through 3.7).

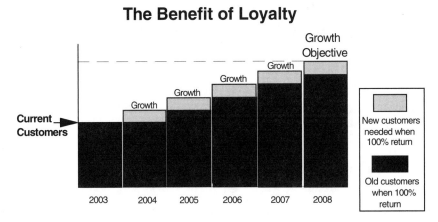

Figure 3.5 A perfect world: 100 percent of customers return.

For example, to achieve its strategic financial plan, Brand X has a five-year growth objective in sales revenue. If all customers returned to buy again, say every four years, then each year the company would have a strong base of returning customers and would only need to attract and sell to a small amount of new customers to meet their growth objective. However, given Brand X's 30 percent loyalty rate and 70 percent defection, another picture quickly emerges (see Figure 3.6).

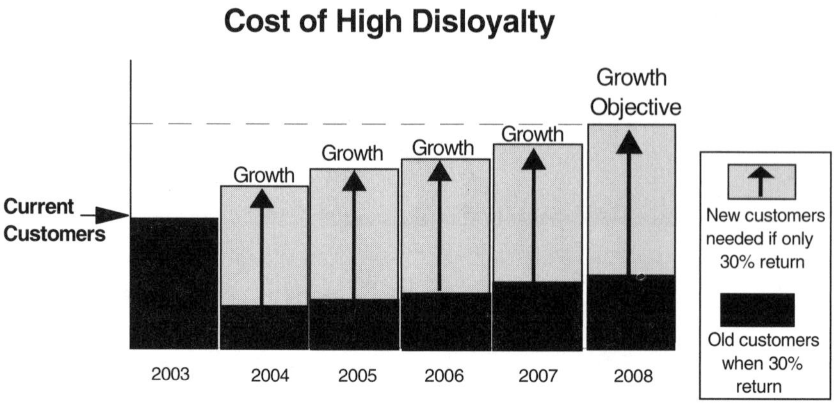

Cost of High Disloyalty

Figure 3.6 The real world: Brand X must capture 70 percent new customers to replace defectors each year, plus attain a growth target.

In this example, rather than start from a strong base of returning customers each year, Brand X must first reset its baseline down to reflect that only 30 percent will return. Before it can sell any "growth" the following year, it must first replace with new customers the 70 percent that defected. Then it must sell an additional amount, primarily also to new customers, to actually grow their business and revenue volumes.

So, how does this relate to their competitors, all of whom have a higher rate of customer loyalty and returning buyers (see Figure 3.7)?

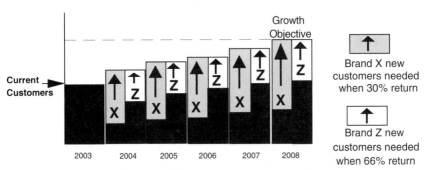

Figure 3.7 Competitive reality: Brand Z needs fewer new customers to attain its growth target.

For Brand Z, a dramatically different financial picture emerges: 66 percent of its former customers return to generate low-cost, high-profit sales. This is a significant competitive advantage over Brand X, which must incur greater expenditures and costs per sale and will have fewer funds available to invest in other areas, such as customer service or research and development. The financial implications of Figures 3.5 through 3.7 are enormous. Even if both firms attain their sales volumes, their cost of sales—and resultant profit and shareholder value—will be dramatically different. That great difference is why customer management and customer-facing processes have become the top levers among business processes (see Figure 3.1), why customer loyalty has risen to #1 on the list of CEO issues (see Figure 3.2), and why customer retention has become the most important element in the management continuum of retain/attract/develop (see Figure 3.3).

So, what are the critical issues associated with a firm's desire to be customer centric and to attain world-class customer loyalty? Another survey reveals an interesting viewpoint on the part of CEOs (see Figure 3.8).

Greatest Obstacles to Customer Orientation

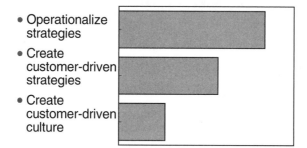

Figure 3.8 Obstacles to attain a customer-focused strategy. Source: ADL survey of more than 130 major U.S. corporations.

Figure 3.8 speaks volumes regarding the level of misunderstanding of what is involved to become customer centric and to manage customer loyalty. Most of the companies surveyed are only starting their journeys, and executives with little or no actual experience believe that their greatest issue will be the implementation of new processes and infrastructure to operationalize a customer strategy. Only slightly less difficult, in their opinion, will be the development of that strategy followed, even less in difficulty, by changes to the culture of the firm.

As the founder of a global practice to transform businesses to be customer centered, and based on our experiences with those companies worldwide, my view is that the chart in Figure 3.8 is literally upside down. The concerns expressed by these managers are correct, but the sequencing of difficulty merely reflects a lack of actual experience. In fact, many respected brands today (such as technology giants Toshiba, Fujitsu, Gateway, and Sun Microsystems) are grappling with the cultural challenges to move from a purely product orientation to product plus service(s) or solutions. Such firms are finding their cultural gaps to be huge and, perhaps, the most difficult issues to handle in the transformation.

We discuss these issues and provide leading-edge, practical approaches to address them later in this book. The chart is relevant here, under *The Case for Action,* because it demonstrates the need for practical, experience-based information to develop and implement customer strategy and deal with the cultural issues. These are not intuitive, and in some cases may actually be counterintuitive. The skills, intuition, and prior experiences of good managers, as seen in Figure 3.8, can be off-the-mark when examined in the light of actual experience and world-class approaches.

As we progress from Part 1 to Part 2, we shift from *why* to improve customer loyalty, and focus instead on the issues regarding actually doing it. The first step to understand *how* to influence or manage customer loyalty and attrition is to examine the drivers of loyalty and defection.

You Are the Customer

You are a customer.

Can you remember when you first became aware of a shift in your own expectations regarding a customer-friendly environment or experience when conducting business?

Was it due to exceptional customer service you received in one environment and then came to desire in others? If you had a great experience when buying or seeking help with a product or service, did that start to establish in your mind the VALUE of receiving customer-focused attention from companies?

Was it due to advertising or news media coverage of dramatic new technologies or services that were being introduced? Did that begin to raise your awareness of what was becoming possible in terms of tailored, personalized products, services, and interactions for an individual consumer?

When you first heard about Internet-enabled personalization introduced by firms such as Amazon.com, or the tailored Web pages available at financial services firms, did you perceive any value in those?

Think about when such customer-focused and customer-friendly capabilities became more common and you began to both hear about the growing trend toward customer-centric products and channels and to also experience them.

What about when you first enjoyed an actual individualized inter-action—perhaps a personalized, targeted recommendation on Amazon.com (e.g., "Others who bought this product also bought the following items."). How did you feel?

And, later, when you dealt with a less customer-focused firm or distribution channel (perhaps your cable provider or a "Select options 1-9" telephone response system), how did you then feel?

Can you remember when you began to value the *benefits you could receive* from extraordinary touchpoint experiences, such as ease of access to information about products or services? Or ease of ordering, receiving, or paying?

What firms with whom you have done business in the past year have become your ideal and preferred vendors? Is it because of their unique product and price, or because of their service and benefits at customer touchpoints?

Over recent years, have your expectations changed from when you were initially excited/delighted by such service? Have these experiences moved from the realm of a pleasant surprise to that of a requirement to deserve your business?

Is it becoming easier to find—and *defect* to—alternate sources that can provide you with such high-value interactions while acquiring their goods/services? Could you be attracted (**stolen**) away to get such benefits, if products and services are relatively equal among different vendors?

■ Might this also be true for *your* customers?

2

Understanding Loyalty: A Pie Pan of Needs

"It's simple, see . . . "

— Ross Perot, U.S. presidential candidate,
on a complex economic issue

4

Product vs.
Service Slices

Customer behavior is highly complex, and the management of loyalty is both an art and science—not easily understood, explained, or practiced. It is not *simple to see*, but a simple analogy can make the topic easier to understand: Imagine a pie pan where each slice represents something specific a customer wants and can impact whether he or she will return again. In Part 2, you examine the current trends in customer behavior and the relative loyalty impacts of the different "needs and wants" slices that can make up a customer loyalty pie (see Figure 4.1).

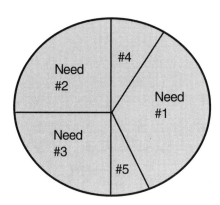

Figure 4.1 The loyalty pie: Customer needs "slices" and their relative impacts.

Corporations typically have an extensive list of customer needs and wants identified and have also surveyed their customers exhaustively regarding *satisfaction* with the firm's performance of those needs. Soon after such a survey, great gnashing of teeth and marshaling of resources takes place to address areas of customer dissatisfaction. But in almost no instances have I seen a firm that also knew WHICH of those expressed customer needs or wants have the most impact on whether customers will buy again and whether bottom-line results will increase.

Businesses often expend precious energy and limited resources trying to address customer satisfaction levels on things that have no correlation between whether they will buy again or leave. The great mistake made almost universally by so-called customer-focused businesses is that they fail to differentiate between customer satisfaction and customer loyalty, and furthermore, between satisfaction or loyalty *measurement* and satisfaction or loyalty *management*.

HEALTHCARE: *Rx* FOR LOYALTY

The CEO of a healthcare network asked me to keynote a conference of hospital executives from around the country. Their theme was "Improving Customer Satisfaction Measurement." The CEO said, "Harvey, I want you to shake them up. Don't be afraid to be controversial."

After he kicked off the conference, the CEO introduced me as a speaker who would both set the tone for their conference and challenge them in their thinking. I stepped to the podium and said, "Well, to begin, you have the wrong theme for your conference!"

As the CEO's mouth fell open, I continued, "Measuring satisfaction is merely somewhat interesting. I think what you really want to do is to manage, not just measure, it. To do that you need more than measures of satisfaction. You need a management system that is driven by those measurements and that will take action based upon your customer surveys and feedback." The CEO's mouth closed and he leaned back in his front row seat. Apparently he liked what he was hearing.

I went on, "But I think what you really want to manage is not customer satisfaction, but customer loyalty. Why do you want satisfied customers? To create happy faces? No. You want satisfied customers in the hope that they will return. What you really want is

HEALTHCARE: *Rx* FOR LOYALTY (continued)

to create loyalty, and the path you have chosen to do that is this conference on customer satisfaction measurement. So, what I'll talk about this morning is how to create and manage customer loyalty by measuring—and having a management system that is driven by—their satisfaction on things that actually DRIVE THEIR LOYALTY."

At that point several hundred attendees visibly relaxed and settled back into their own auditorium seats. We had embarked on a valuable conference for them and for their customers.

I know you have heard that point before—customer satisfaction is not the same as customer loyalty. But what does it really mean?

First, it means that you must conduct market research to understand the customer needs that make up their loyalty pie before you can construct meaningful satisfaction surveys. Such research should be focused to identify (isolate) those wants and needs that will make customers leave if not provided, plus other wants and needs that could differentiate your firm and attract new customers if offered by you. Those are the loyalty drivers that should appear on your subsequent satisfaction surveys.

Second, it means you must understand more than mere market satisfaction with those needs. You must understand that the relative importance and loyalty-driving impacts of those will vary across different groups of customers. The satisfaction with a specific item can have a far different impact on loyalty for one group than the same satisfaction level does on another group. We cover that issue in depth in the next chapter on segmentation as we discuss how to separate customers into groups with not only similar needs, but also similar priorities and weightings of their needs.

Finally, it means that loyalty is a customer behavior that is influenced by many different factors that cannot be easily identified or captured in a single satisfaction survey. For example, loyalty can be driven by:

· The price of products vs. the customers' perception of value.

· Product attributes and how well they match customer needs and wants.

· Service attributes and how well they meet customer needs and wants.

· Prices, products, or services vs. competitive positioning.

· Brand image, particularly where style, safety, or security are important.

· Economic factors, such as recessionary eras, that dampen spending and change buying behavior.

· Legislative factors that impact access, availability, or prices.

Many of the above are out of your firm's control, and balancing the ones that are within your control can seem daunting and beyond your capabilities. However, you must first walk before you can run and most companies today are at a *crawl-level* of competency regarding customer loyalty. So, before we discuss innovative concepts to enable your firm to run the loyalty race, here are some basic (walking) points regarding the drivers of customer loyalty that are almost universally misunderstood. We limit the discussion to more controllable factors such as products and services, rather than the global economy or national and regional legislative impacts.

Basic Drivers of Customer Loyalty

To begin, most major companies, such as the previously mentioned automotive example, attained their past successes and current brand image based on a high-quality product. They built their customer loyalty and generated return business with the features, benefits, and price of their products. In fact, when I joined IBM many years ago, an emphasis on features, benefits, and price was the backbone of sales training for any big firm. Those sales techniques were employed primarily within a single channel—in IBM's case, blue-suited salespersons.

If a typical customer segment (a group of customers with a common set of demographics) had been analyzed, a pie chart during that era would have primarily depicted that *product elements* (features, benefits, price) determined most buying decisions. Successful firms of the 1960s, '70s, '80s, and '90s knew that very well, perhaps too well. As discussed earlier, that thinking continues to be the filter that executives use today when viewing their customers' behavior (such as a 70 percent defection rate).

However, the actual environment and typical customer loyalty pie pan/chart today are quite different (see Figure 4.2).

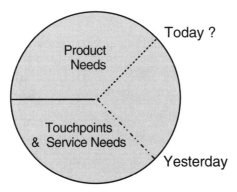

Figure 4.2 The loyalty pie: Impact of product vs. service needs.

The chart in Figure 4.2 is key to understanding the current issues of customer attrition and customer loyalty or retention. It depicts the reason that customer retention is now the #1 management issue of CEOs, and it is a logical culmination of the recent global shift from product to service in business strategy. Companies now increasingly compete and attract customers away from competitors based on their ability to differentiate relatively similar product lines with a service-based value proposition.

Ten years ago, a pie chart of the customer needs and wants that drove buying behavior and loyalty would have skewed the weighting predominantly toward the product-related attributes of a firm. Today, that skew is dramatically tilted away from product impact and weighted more toward service. Note: This assumes that products among competitors are relatively similar, of acceptable quality, and meet customers' minimum needs. It does not mean that products, product quality, or product attributes are no longer important. In an era of high product quality, these have simply become less of a differentiator or a means to insure customer retention and loyalty.

During creative visioning focus groups, customers who have defected often state that, although they liked a firm's products, when the service manager moved to a different brand or retailer then so did the customer. Others report that, although they were happy with a brand, they left because their customer service touchpoint person had moved to a new firm. The "loyal" customers followed, but their loyalty was due to the perceived value they received during touchpoint interactions, not the product.

Who stole those customers??

Interestingly, many of these customers had responded favorably to customer satisfaction surveys regarding the performance of various attributes of the product, and even some elements of service, but those firms missed the mark by not also asking what things were most important to their loyalty. When another firm differentiated itself (in this case by hiring the service manager), those *happy* customers defected. So much for the value of high satisfaction on typical customer surveys—or of conferences on satisfaction measurement.

Why is this important? Because many firms today are trying to make customer needs and wants their focus. They are investing in research to better understand their customers and to use the customers' viewpoints and requirements to design the firm's capabilities, infrastructure, and measures of success (see Figure 4.3). If a business cannot discern between the actual drivers of customer buying behavior and a vast potpourri of customer needs and wants that don't drive behavior, their investments will be wasted.

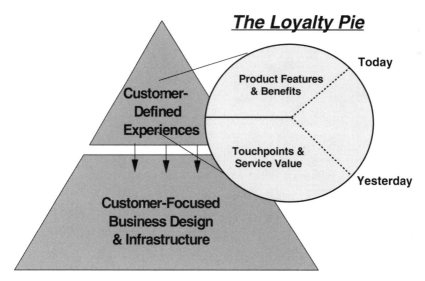

Figure 4.3 What are the levers for your success: Product? Service? How are you using them to design your business?

Figure 4.3 places the customer loyalty pie into a context for business improvement. By placing the customer needs at the top of the model, as the design requirements for the bottom portion, business capabilities and infrastructure can be envisioned to bring the firm's delivery capabilities into alignment with the needs of their customers. For purposes of this book, it is important to understand that only loyalty-driving needs should be in your design, and they are dramatically changing. Saying, "Have a nice day," is no longer an acceptable surrogate for finding out what the customers want and giving it to them (see Figure 4.4).

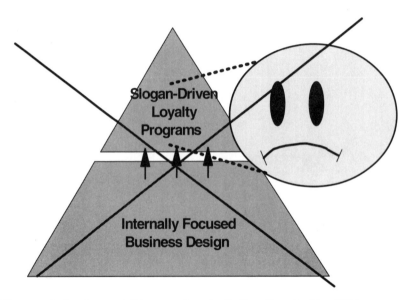

Figure 4.4 Beyond "Have a nice day": Goodbye to the 1990s.

While the phrase "Have a nice day" epitomized the depth (and sincerity) of most customer-focused initiatives of the 1990s, companies must now move dramatically beyond such shallow (and inexpensive) vehicles to attract and retain market share.

You Are the Customer

You are a customer. What do you think most drives loyalty today?

What drives/influences yours? What determines whether *you* return to a given vendor? What can attract you to defect?

To what extent is your loyalty to a firm or your defection impacted by the following:

- The perceived quality of goods or service products that you have received.
- The features and benefits of a firm's product line vs. those of its competitors.
- The price that you paid vs. the prices available from other sources.
- The brand image or reputation of a company.
- The ease of use of a firm's product.
- The ease of access to information to enable your buying decision.
- The customer experience you had when shopping or buying there.
- The consultative sales advice you received to ensure you get what you need.

- How well they understood you and proposed only things that fit your needs.
- The customer experience you had when receiving your purchase.
- The customer experience you had when learning to use your purchase.
- The customer experience you had when paying for your purchase.
- The customer experience you had when receiving post-sales service.
- The customer experience you had when you complained.
- The customer return policy you experienced when returning an item.
- Whether they know you when you come in.
- Whether they remember your history and what you have previously ordered.
- Whether they have a consistent, customer-focused culture.
- The presence of alternate channels that you can use to access products or information at your choice or option (phone, store, fax, Internet, kiosk, dealers, and so on).
- The consistency of their channels regarding content, format, ease of use, vendor information, and so on.

How many of the above were service related rather than product related?

Are satisfaction surveys always a good indicator and/or predictor of your own loyalty? Have you ever been dissatisfied with a firm (or completed their survey and checked "dissatisfied" on one or more questions) but continued to do business there? Why? Was it because the things with which you were surveyed were not the major factors in how you decide where to buy?

Have you ever been satisfied with a firm (or completed their survey and checked "satisfied") but then left and did not return? Why? Was it because the things with which you were satisfied were not also the final determinates of where you decide to buy?

How could a firm that you do business with today insure you remain their loyal customer? What could they do to learn what drives your buying behavior?

What should they do with that information?

■ What about *your* customers? What are you doing?

5

Customer Segmentation and Targeting

onsumer and commercial customer behaviors are influenced by a myriad of factors including an extensive set of needs and wants. However, the degree of impact on their loyalty by a specific need or want can vary greatly from customer to customer. Something that is one person's absolute requirement can, for another person, be merely a *nice-to-have*. What attracts one customer to defect to a new vendor may have little effect on another customer. What is a business to do? How can a firm effectively be responsive to such an extensive customer wish list? If the firm cannot afford to address all of them, which of the needs should receive its focus and limited resources?

The first challenge is to define the word *loyalty* for your business, based on how you wish to compete. For example, a bank might define loyalty as *repeat customers*, such as those who return when their certificates of deposit expire to purchase replacements. Or loyalty for a bank could mean having a major *share of a customer's wallet*, e.g., when a household has three financial services products such as a CD, a mortgage, and a savings account and all are at the same bank. It could also refer to *highly profitable customers* who expand their scope of business beyond products and return for other fee-based services, such as consulting or financial advice. Or loyalty could refer to the type of *buyer who responds to values other than lowest price* such as a firm's service quality or relationships. How a firm plans to make money will drive its specific definition of the desired type of "customer loyalty."

An extremely successful auto dealership in North America, for example, has high prices. Its strategy for customer loyalty is not to target *customers who return if they get a low price*, but rather those who live within 20 miles and come back for their (high-profit-margin) parts and maintenance service and who value—and will return for—personalized treatment over price. Other businesses have their own strategies for making money, which define what they mean by loyalty.

Next, you must define the drivers of the type of loyalty you desire, but from your target customers' points of view; and understand that those customers will group into segments with *very different needs* or with similar needs but *different priorities* (see Figure 5.1).

What are your priorities for a business lunch?

Restaurant Attributes	North America Priority	Europe & Asia Priority
• Fast service	# 1	# 6
• Good location	2	5
• Fair price	3	3
• Good food	4	1
• Courteous service	5	4
• Ambiance	# 6	# 2

Figure 5.1 Segmentation 101: Find out what's important and give it to them! Source: Adapted from responses by attendees at IBM seminar, La Hulpe, Belgium.

The needs of different groups may be similar, but their priorities (as seen in Figure 5.1) can be quite different and require unique customer experience engineering to create a loyal relationship and retain them. This example of classic needs-based segmentation was used to demonstrate to a large group of professionals the reality of customer loyalty management. To do this, the group's members were challenged to think about when they were customers themselves. The scenario was that they were to envision the ideal restaurant for a business luncheon appointment and identify the attributes that would most determine their decision to select that site for lunch.

The group was comprised of business people from around the world. There were representatives from Asia (Japan, Hong Kong, and Korea), but primarily the session was attended by people from North America (U.S. and Canada) and Western Europe (Britain, France, Belgium, Netherlands, Germany, and Italy).

First, they identified the critical activities or events that would occur related to their luncheon. They named steps such as identifying the restaurants in that geographic area, making a reservation, driving there, parking, being seated, reviewing the menu, ordering, and other activities related to the meal.

Then they envisioned how they could ideally receive value or benefits during each of those moments as well as their minimum requirements or expectations.

Finally, after their collective needs and wants were distilled down into a few major topics, the people were each asked to prioritize the list of needs.

The results are displayed in Figure 5.1. This very mixed audience, from dissimilar cultural and geographic backgrounds, had similar needs and wants. All wanted an appropriate ambiance for their business meeting. All wanted good service. All wanted good food. And so forth.

However, the importance of those elements, and their relative priorities, varied greatly between the people, who could then easily be categorized into two groups, with different loyalty-driving requirements. As it turned out, the two needs-based groups also had another factor in common within each group—geography.

Needs-based Group A (primarily composed of North Americans) placed their highest priority upon *speedy service*, while placing much less emphasis on *ambiance* when compared to the other items on the list. In fact, it was rated as least important.

Needs-based Group B (primarily composed of Europeans and Asians) placed extremely high emphasis on *ambience*, and while they also considered *speedy service* to be needed, it was considered the least important item on their list.

What does this mean (beyond confirming your suspicions about Americans and food)? It means that within your desired customers, you must not only understand the needs that make up the slices of their loyalty pie, but also the size of each slice. Because to attract and retain different customers, it may require dramatically different investments in infrastructure or quite different utilizations of common infrastructure.

Interactions with banks, automobile manufacturers, and (in this case) restaurants can provide a great backdrop to demonstrate and help you understand this customer loyalty concept.

AUTOMOTIVE: WHY ALL CARS AREN'T BLACK

When I was with IBM, we often used automotive experiences as analogies in classes for our global network of consultants. My favorite was to share a customer-visioning focus group experience from England. A European auto manufacturer (not Brand X from Chapter 1) wanted to understand the customer segments that bought their brand and also how to appeal to another segment that consistently bought (were loyal to) another brand. Our client's brand had a public image for being a conservative company and, understandably, their loyal customers seemed to be of a similar ilk. The questions to be addressed were: "Why do some customers buy from us and other customers buy from our competitor? How do we keep our existing customers and also attract (**steal away**) those of our competitor?"

To begin the study, we held customer focus groups with the client's own loyal customers and had them define their vision of an ideal automaker. It is common for marketing research firms in the UK to provide food and drink, including alcohol, on a table at the back of the room. However, during the course of the evening, when offered beverages, not a single customer of the client selected alcohol. After all, they were driving home after the event. The client's customers repeatedly stated a very cautious, often self-deprecating, view of themselves and of the companies with which they preferred to do business.

When asked how they should be treated after buying several vehicles from a single dealership, their reply was that they would expect no special treatment and would prefer to "wait their turn" for subsequent service.

AUTOMOTIVE: WHY ALL CARS AREN'T BLACK (continued)

When asked the most important attributes of an automobile, they clearly preferred a safe, well-constructed car that had good brakes and protected the occupants in a crash.

Later, we held identical competitive sessions with another buying segment that seemed to prefer and be more loyal to the client's main competitor. When offered beverages, every participant from the competitive brand not only selected alcohol, but during the course of the evening several folks took up positions closer to the drink table. In fact, we actually ran out of beer halfway into each session.

When asked how they should be treated if they purchased several vehicles at the same dealership, they forcefully said they should be immediately moved to the front of the line (queue) when they arrived for service. They were indignant at the idea of being relegated to "wait their turn" and felt that their loyalty to the brand should be returned in kind.

When asked the attributes of the ideal car, they said (with somewhat slurred speech) not to provide a crash cage around them for protection. Instead, they required great handling and maneuverability and "Let the b***ds try to hit me!" Nothing was said about brakes at all.

The sessions strongly suggested needs-based, buyer-behavior segmentation. The expressed personal values, needs, and wants that drive the behavior of one major market segment were diametrically different from those of the second set of potential buyers—safety and security were highly valued by one group versus the high-speed

AUTOMOTIVE: WHY ALL CARS AREN'T BLACK (continued)

handling and performance strongly preferred by the other. Even their beverage choices suggested that different personal values existed between the two groups. We had developed valuable insights and hypotheses regarding how to keep customers from defecting, as well as how to attract new customers. More extensive, statistically valid surveys later confirmed them.

The successful firm today must understand how such needs and wants vary across market segments and then tailor product offerings, services, and interactions to appeal to each desired customer group. Failure to do so can cause a firm to miss a potential opportunity to attract new customers. Worse, it can also provide savvy competitors who segment and target the market with a great advantage to **steal away** a firm's existing customers.

You Are the Customer

What about when you are the customer?

What is your definition of loyalty? When do you most feel that you are being loyal? Is it when you return to buy as a repeat customer for a replacement item? Or, is it when you return and buy additional, yet very different items, giving them an increased share of your total wallet spending?

When you do that, what is it that they provide of such value that they win your loyalty? If they did not provide that, would you be more likely to leave/defect and be **stolen away** as their customer?

Do you think your needs are much the same as other folks'? Or are your needs and wants sometimes quite different from some of your friends or neighbors? Do you know other people who do not share your views and don't want exactly the same things that you want? Have you ever heard someone complain or say they will not do business with a firm because of something they wanted, but you simply did not share that feeling?

■ What about *your* customers? Do you think one size fits all of *them*?

3

Integrating Two Views: Opportunity vs. Risk

I'm told that the Chinese have one word that means both opportunity and risk. In customer loyalty management, there is a similar word: touchpoints.

6

Opportunity: The Customer View

ustomer touchpoints interact with a firm's people, processes, and channels and represent the greatest opportunities to impact their loyalty with non-product-related initiatives. The biggest payoff is to engineer a consistent, long-running, personalized customer experience across the myriad processes, channels, and organizations within the business.

For example, consider interactions with your company from a customer's point of view:

· First, each interaction is approached by the customer from a
  mindset based on who the customer is and which respective
  "needs-based" segment he or she occupies. Depending on the
  segment, each customer will have a specific set of needs that
  will drive his or her loyalty and determine whether he or she will
  return again (see Figure 6.1).

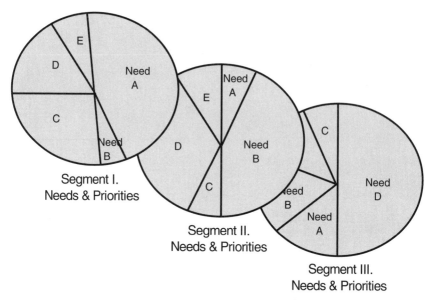

Figure 6.1 Segmentation: Groups of customers with similar needs
and priorities.

· Needs may vary greatly between segments, or they may be
  the same yet have dramatically different weightings in terms
  of impact on their buying behavior. In Figure 6.1, some

financial services customers (Segment I) have a greater need for *detailed information* (Need A) than they do for *ease of use* (Need B) when using an automated teller machine or telephone response system. Other people (Segment II) have little patience to navigate such complexity and value *ease of use* more than *detailed information*. Both groups want ease of use and an appropriate level of detail, but each group has a different set of priorities that would cause them to stay or defect. Knowledge of each segment's loyalty-driving needs provides a powerful enabler for the firm to retain existing customers within a segment and attract new ones. We discuss how to identify those needs in Chapter 9, "What They Need: Customer Visioneering."

· Second, customers also approach each touchpoint interaction based on where they currently reside in their customer life cycle. The term *life cycle* is commonly used in business—particularly in financial services—and company products or services are often designed and developed based on the major stages of customers' lives (see Figure 6.2).

Where the customers have progressed in their lives can have a great impact on their current needs, so banks keep track of life events in order to make targeted offers with a high probability of matching a customer's requirements at that point in time.

Life Events:
★ Birth
★ School
★ Employment
★ Marriage
★ Children
★ Purchase Home
★ Relocate
★ Retire
★ Death

Figure 6.2 Customer life cycle: Based on major life events.

The important thing to remember here is that in addition to product or service offerings, touchpoint experiences can also be engineered to appeal to each customer's changing needs as they progress through those life cycle stages. What customers experience during touchpoints can not only provide great value, but can also differentiate the firm and generate loyalty.

· Third, to do this, your business must go farther into the minds of the customers and respond to another form of "customer life cycle" that is also occurring. In fact, I prefer to call the previous factors Life Events, rather than a customer life cycle, because this second customer life-cycle phenomenon is truly recurring and cyclical and applies more specifically to the customer relationship. No matter which personal Life Event is taking place in the background (with the probable exception of their birth and death), this repeating customer cycle greatly impacts their needs at a particular moment (see Figure 6.3).

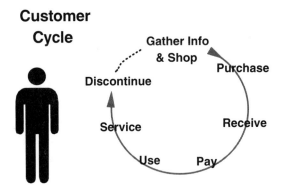

Figure 6.3 Customer life cycle: Based on an actual stage of a customer relationship.

Each touchpoint in Figure 6.3 represents a company's interaction with its customer's process, such as shopping, buying, paying, or securing post-sale service. And this is true whether the transaction is with a commercial customer (a company) or an individual consumer. In that context, each touchpoint also offers the business an opportunity to find out what the customer wants during the interaction that will make the customer's processes more efficient and/or more effective.

This is a major value proposition or lever for customer loyalty and attrition management. Although your products and services are relatively equal to your competitors', your firm can provide great value, differentiate your business, and create loyal customers by making your customer-facing processes, channels, and touch-points the ideal inputs to your customers' processes. At that critical juncture you can turn a "moment of truth" for you into a "moment of value" for your customer.

From the perspective of your customer, there are an incredible number of possible instances to do that, each of which represents both opportunity and risk for your business (see Figure 6.4). Figure 6.4 presents a simple, graphic depiction of the business relationship between a customer and the potential contact points with a business. Within that picture are countless opportunities to provide extraordinary, differentiating customer value—and as many potential chances to disappoint and even lose a customer.

If you look closely, you will see that the centerline of Figure 6.4 is actually a version of the customer life cycle from Figure 6.3, but in order to illustrate a point, the contents have been depicted on a horizontal timeline rather than in a closed loop. The vertical arrows also call out that as customers progress along the timeline of life-cycle activities, they can interact with a company using many different channels. In fact, customers may actually skip back and forth between those channels as they move across the timeline. There are two very different, yet tightly linked, customer opportunities (and risks) being depicted—one is the horizontal message of how a customer travels across a timeline for an ongoing relationship; the other is the vertical depiction of how at any point on the timeline the customer experience can occur via many different points of multi-channel contact.

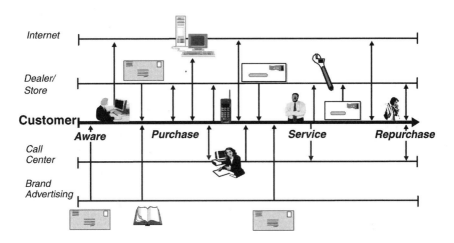

Figure 6.4 The objective: A consistent, horizontal and vertical customer experience. Source: Adapted from work by Terry G. Vavra and Douglas R. Pruden of Marketing Metrics, Inc., Paramus, New Jersey.

What customers on this chart want are:

- A horizontal experience—a single, long-running relationship.

- A vertical experience—a consistent experience, irrespective of the channel used.

We examine these two aspects in depth and one at a time.

First, let's look at a single, long-running customer relationship. Look at Figure 6.4 horizontally, and observe the potential contacts made with a firm as a customer seeks information about a product, then negotiates a price and purchases it, then pays and takes delivery, and later secures service. What is not captured is that this cycle repeats itself with every subsequent purchase. In fact, at any given moment a customer may be on different points on such a timeline regarding many different products—some purchased, some paid for, some being serviced, and so on. What customers often want is for your knowledge of them at each of these interactions to be captured and continued forward, so that subsequent contact points are enabled with full information about the relationship history, i.e., what the customer has ordered in the past, their preferences, their service record, their prior contacts for information or problem resolution, and so on. And they want that relationship enterprise-wide.

The challenge is to provide your employees at contact points across the timeline with a single, long-running, enterprise-wide history of each customer to enable a consistent, personalized customer experience.

The reality that customers often experience is quite different, because they are asked to repeat information they have provided during previous contacts. For example, "I've been a customer here for years; how many times do I have to give you this?" Or worse, customers are asked to restate their question or problem every time they are transferred during a single telephone contact: "Why are you asking me this? I just covered that in great detail with the person who transferred me to you!"

Due to specialization in businesses, one function (or product division) along the timeline may have little or no carryover and access to information regarding a customer's history or relationships with the other areas. The accounts receivable function of an IBM division that maintained customers' typewriters once (long ago) sent a threatening collection letter to Ross Perot, then CEO of EDS, for the maintenance contract of a single typewriter, apparently unaware he was one of the largest customers of IBM's computer division. He reportedly said he wasn't worried, because there weren't enough trucks in the entire country to pick up all the equipment he leased from IBM.

Amazingly, with all the business intelligence and customer data that is amassed today, that type of story remains true for major companies. Banks, for example, often have credit card customers who receive treatment from that function of the bank that is totally inappropriate (and blind) to the overall institutional relationship—the customer may have millions deposited or invested up the hall in other areas of the bank, yet receives irritating correspondence, mundane service response, and irrational fees.

Before we move on from the topic of the horizontal, long-running relationship opportunities in Figure 6.4, consider the segment of automotive customers who said that if they bought several vehicles (sales department interactions), they expected special treatment when they returned for maintenance (service department interactions). Although this group was particularly self-serving, they provide a real-life example that many customers expect or demand that you know who they are, their history with you, their needs or preferences, and then treat them accordingly.

The second message in Figure 6.4 is the vertical complexity, risks, and opportunities associated with a customer's life cycle and touchpoint experiences. As customers move along the horizontal timeline on the chart, they have many different options regarding the touchpoint access channels used. The chart depicts vertically only a few of the myriad possible vehicles with which a customer and a company interact. The list could be expanded to include the following and still be incomplete:

- Company retail outlet sales personnel
- Company retail outlet customer service, complaint, and returns personnel
- Third-party distributors and franchisees
- Factory sales representatives
- Centralized telephone contact center personnel
- Outsourced, third-party customer service or help lines
- Automated voice response units
- Kiosks
- Internet online Web sites
- Mail
- Advertising media, and so forth

For businesses, the challenge is to enable employees at each point of contact with the information to provide a single, ongoing customer relationship as the customer proceeds along the time-line, and also to provide consistency across many potential channel contact points at that moment.

If an.existing customer is shopping and contacts a firm for product information, say via the Internet, then his or her subsequent interactions that utilize any other channel should be consistent. If an Internet site, an advertisement, or a mailed promotion says there is a special offer with 15 percent off certain products, then when the customer later goes into a store or calls a telephone contact center, those folks should also be aware of it. Sounds simple. It isn't. Businesses are seldom able to provide changes and updates to all channels simultaneously. It is quite difficult to revise all the data sources a retail sales person uses, plus those at the telephone call centers, not to mention the Internet—all of which can have unique and insular management, staffs, procedures, manuals, and brochures. That's the Company View of the risks of multiple channels.

The Customer View: "I received a mailing that said you were making a great special offer for a limited time. I called your telephone contact center to order it, but they said they weren't aware of it, and that sometimes there were Internet-only specials and I should check there. I looked on your Web site, but there wasn't any mention of it, so I clicked on *locate the nearest available store*. Now here I am at your store; can someone *please* tell me how to do this?"

Ensuring a consistent experience across all channels regarding your own product information can be a challenge, but with focus and investment it can be managed relatively easier than the next issue: consistent knowledge of each customer, vertically across the channels shown in Figure 6.4. Customers expect to deal with a single enterprise and to have each functional area (sales, billing, service) carry forward and share information about them. Beyond that, there must also be sharing across and between the channels. Each contact by a customer should be handled as a customer contact to the enterprise, not just to the channel. The fact that a customer has reached your call center is data that should not be held hostage within the center, but should be available to all subsequent contact points, including other channels.

If a current customer has a Web interaction to configure a new ZOT 12 automobile and later calls that brand's toll-free telephone number for additional information, data on both events should be available to the sales representative when the customer subsequently goes to a dealer. Not only should the product information the customer receives at each contact point be consistent within the channels, but knowledge about the customer and his or her interactions with the firm should also be consistent across all possible channel contact points and along the timeline.

If you put the two together, both the horizontal and vertical implications of Figure 6.4, true customer relationship and loyalty management can be attained. With that business model, a consistently winning customer experience is enabled as customers proceed along the timeline and as they potentially jump between different channels at different points.

For example, imagine that a family has a history of buying ZOT automobiles. There are two in the family garage, and a third, older vehicle is driven by their son or daughter in college. A family member goes onto the Internet and views the new ZOT 12, then requests a brochure by mail. Perhaps he or she later goes to a local dealer for a test drive. If you were the ZOT Corporation, wouldn't you want the salesperson to know the history of this repeat, loyal, high-profit customer? What about the customer's contacts with ZOT via several channels? Wouldn't you want these and subsequent contacts to be a continuing, single relationship that is built on the value added at each contact, rather than starting over at each contact? What if the customer then called your toll-free telephone number and asked for something, say a ZOT logo ball cap or some extraordinary information? Wouldn't you want the telephone customer service person to be enabled with information regarding this customer so he or she would be handled in a business-value appropriate way?

What if that customer called your area service rep and said your warranty expired the preceding Friday for one of their (three . . . and a fourth is being considered) ZOT automobiles, and then the transmission failed over the weekend? Wouldn't you want the service side of your organization to know the sales value of the customer when considering whether to make an exception or concession? What if your employees do not have this information available cross-functionally and cross-channel? Do you see why customer touchpoint interactions today represent both risk and opportunity?

You Are the Customer

You are a customer.

What do you want when you have repeat interactions with a business? Do you place a high value on dealing with someone who has excellent knowledge of their firm's products? Do you want them to advise you on the best fit for your needs? Is a highly skilled *transactional* relationship what you want?

For example, when you go to a major brand outlet of electronic products and audio/video equipment, you may wish to receive expert transactional support. You may want a knowledgeable salesperson to ask you questions to understand your needs and then propose their best product to fit your needs. Salesperson: "I understand you want to buy a television. Tell me how and where you will use it. How big is the cabinet or space where you will place it? What colors are your existing audio and video components that it must match? What brands of equipment do you have, so that a universal remote controller can operate them all, including the new television?"

How would you feel about that transaction? Would it feel consultative and oriented to your needs? Would that be sufficient to insure you would return, if the product is okay?

Imagine you return to the same store three months later to purchase a VCR to go with the television you recently bought there. In such a transactional (vs. long-running) relationship, even a highly skilled, consultative salesperson must handle your next visit for the VCR in the following manner:

Salesperson: "I understand you want to buy a VCR. Tell me about how and where you will use it. How big is the cabinet or space in which you will place it? What colors are your television and other audio/video components that the VCR must match?" And so on.

Again, that is a transactional relationship, albeit a consultative one. How would you feel about this second transactional experience?

Suppose you return to that same store for a DVD player to attach to the television and VCR that you have now purchased there, and a salesperson asks, "Tell me about . . ."

Now, imagine you return yet a fourth time, for wireless headphones, but now the salesperson has access to knowledge about you and your prior history. The salesperson says, "No problem, Mr./Ms./Mrs. (*insert your name*). I see here that you have the Acme widescreen 45" television with the Big X VCR and a matching DVD player. You know, Acme makes great wireless headphones, but they don't work well with Big X components. There's another company that has a headphone that's actually less expensive than Acme's and it works well with both brands of equipment you have installed. We don't have it in stock, but I'll order it for you, and we'll waive the shipping charges because you have bought so much from us in the past."

That's not a transactional relationship, that's a long-running one. Your contact person is enabled with knowledge of you, your past purchases, your preferences, and most importantly your value to that business as a repeat customer.

How would that make you feel? If prices and products were equal to competition, would the potential for such a relationship attract your business?

If you already had such a knowledge-based relationship, and other firms offered similar products, how likely would it be that you would leave and establish a new (transactional—they don't know you yet) relationship?

How easily could you be **stolen away**?

- What about *your* customers? Do you know them? Does each employee at every point of contact have the capability to access (*security-controlled* and *business-role-appropriate*) customer information? Do you provide a single, long-running relationship? Is knowledge of your customers carried forward from transaction to transaction for a learning relationship?

- Is knowledge of them shared cross-functionally so that customer-facing sales, billing, collections, and service personnel all understand the relationship, history, and value of the customer?

- Are your customers' experiences consistent across your channels and alternative contact points?

- Are your customer touchpoint interactions being fully leveraged as opportunities to improve and drive customer loyalty? What if you were your customer? What would it feel like to do business with your firm?

- How easily could your customers be **stolen away** by a competitor? What should you be doing differently?

7

Risk: The Company Culture

From the onset, every customer-focused project is exposed to major differences in how the company sees things, versus the customers' view, that can completely destroy the potential benefit of the investment.

The ideal way to ensure a winning customer experience is to design the touchpoints from the outside-in with the customers' input. In Chapter 6 we discussed potential opportunities from doing this and the risks of *not* doing it. However, there are even *greater risks* from trying this but doing it poorly—which is a typical result of a well-intentioned customer initiative being unraveled by company culture.

What are channel touchpoints, exactly? From the company perspective these are almost always viewed as distribution channels, i.e., their channels are vehicles to *distribute or push* products and services to the marketplace. From the customer point of view, however, these are actually customer vehicles to *access* the firm's products, services, and information. One point of view's *distribution* channels are another's *access* channels. And that only begins to call out how companies and customers see things differently.

This phenomenon is present in virtually all industries, but perhaps a bank can best provide an example where we all are customers and demonstrate how a different point of view can prevent an ideal relationship between a company and the customer (see Figure 7.1).

Today, the typical bank's viewpoint, as depicted in Figure 7.1, can also be applied to other industries. The culture, perspective, and operational strategy for nearly all companies is that *touchpoint interactions* with customers occur primarily via that firm's distribution vehicles: retail stores, the Internet, telephone call centers, and the like. A bank would more specifically include branches and ATMs. Additionally, from a major bank's perspective, its business is comprised of multiple, stand-alone, product-focused business units (or silos, in common business parlance). Each of these is generally treated as a business in its own right, and although they might have customers in common, they typically have little else, including shared information about the customer.

Bank Viewpoint:
A Product-Based, Distribution Strategy

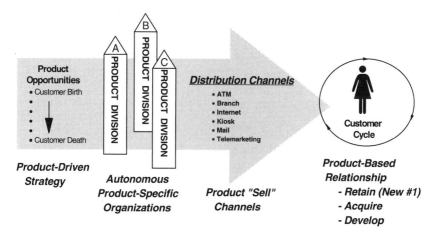

Figure 7.1 What is the greatest exposure to customer loyalty? Culture I.

Each business unit normally has its own set of products, such as credit cards, and a unique, proprietary relationship with its customers. The business units all utilize distribution channels (branches, ATMs, Internet, telephone contact centers, voice response units, and so on) whereby products and services are distributed/pushed out to the marketplace, however, there is often contention and resistance to share the infrastructure that supports those. From the point of view of the independent business units, they are each unique and require specialized infrastructure. The organization, processes, culture, and even the language used within the bank are relentlessly designed and practiced from this inside-out, product-house-focus point of view. Customers are viewed within the context of both life events and a customer life cycle as seen from the bank's perspective (see Figure 7.1). As discussed earlier, beyond major life events, the internal, company view of a customer relationship management cycle has also recently changed from *acquire, develop and retain* to *retain, develop, and acquire.*

Finally, the bank sees customer segmentation as a means to divide customers into groupings with common attributes, but from an internal viewpoint of "the value of the customer" and also "customers with common bank products." It is from that business model and point of view that banks attempt to develop programs to improve customer retention and loyalty.

But what is the actual customer point of view that will determine his or her reaction to the bank's initiatives? What value system will we customers use to assess the bank and determine the success or failure of its efforts? That customer perspective, unfortunately, can be quite different from that of the bank (see Figure 7.2).

Let's look at the exact same relationship, but from a customer's point of view. To begin, customers see their relationship with a bank (or your business) occur during touchpoint interactions with that firm's access channels, not distribution channels. An ATM, branch office, or telephone contact center are all vehicles for customers to access or acquire products, services, and information. When a bank, or any business, designs these for ease of pushing/ distributing goods—rather than from the customer's viewpoint as a means to ideally access those products—they have missed a major opportunity to delight and retain customers. A significant, strategic opportunity (and investment benefit) has been unrealized due to company culture and an inside-out viewpoint.

Customer Viewpoint:
A Needs-Based, Access Strategy

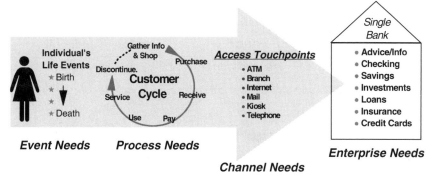

Figure 7.2 What is the greatest exposure to customer loyalty? Culture II.

CONSUMER ELECTRONICS: DON'T CALL US, WE'LL CALL YOU

As an example, I often speak at professional conferences and conduct management briefings with the executive teams of corporations. I was invited to meet with the top management of a well-known brand in Asia, at a remote site away from their headquarters, and decided to take my LED projector to share some charts with them from my laptop. En route, I made a call on a client in Dallas, Texas, and then stayed at a Dallas–Ft. Worth airport hotel, prior to my flight to Asia. While in my room, I tested my laptop projector only to find that it no longer worked.

The logo on the projector was that of a major, well-known brand, so I called the manufacturer to locate their local U.S. service center. With luck, I hoped to have the unit repaired before my flight the following

CONSUMER ELECTRONICS: DON'T CALL US, WE'LL CALL YOU (continued)

evening. When I contacted their U.S. toll-free customer contact center and asked the location of their nearest service location, they were unable to help. They said their "customer service" system was not set up that way, to take a query from a customer and then answer it. Instead, they wanted me to tell them my postal zip code. I was in a Dallas hotel and didn't know the postal code. They were unmoved by my plight and said that without that code there was absolutely no way they could tell me, a customer, where THEIR service centers were located in Texas. In other words, what they had was a *distribution* system, set up to push information out that was organized by the postal codes to which they wanted to sell goods and services. A great distribution system, in the guise of customer service.

To resolve this, I utilized their telephone call center and Internet Web site to get the name of their global executive of marketing. I called his corporate office and told his secretary that a representative of a Fortune 500 firm was about to speak to senior executives in the projector firm's Asian marketplace. Unless I received help within 24 hours, the Asian execs would be seeing technologies from another company. He immediately got on the telephone and, suffice it to say, I arrived in Asia with a working projector.

They may not have been organized around my point of view or access needs as a customer, but luckily I understood theirs as distributors.

They did not have what I needed at that touchpoint: a means to locate and access their service center. What we had was an example of how company and customer viewpoints can conflict on what a customer touchpoint is about—distribution versus access.

Chapter 7
Risk: The Company Culture

Beyond the access-versus-distribution issue, customers want a single, enterprise-wide relationship with a firm. They do not see themselves as being a customer of a half-dozen separate entities. In other words, the customers of Bank One want to deal with one bank, not several autonomous silos. When banks, or other businesses, hold customer information hostage within individual departments, they miss the benefits of offering the customer a unique, single, enterprise-wide relationship that could differentiate themselves. The typical bank's autonomous product-house orientation adds millions to their costs due to silos with overlapping, but unshared call centers, Web resources, billing systems, and customer databases. Plus, each of the business units attempt to provide a silo-specific interface to confused customers who believe they are dealing with a single bank.

Additionally, customers see a very different customer-relationship cycle (see Figure 7.2) than that envisioned by the bank (see Figure 7.1). Customers perceive the life cycle from their own viewpoint while shopping, purchasing, paying, and so on and have little empathy with bank attempts to instead acquire, develop, and retain them. This causes a major conflict in how banks (and your company) design touchpoint interactions and the customer-facing processes and channels that support them. Consider this: at every touchpoint interaction, the company's processes are interacting with the customer's processes—but they are designed from the perspective of the company's process.

The following simple yet powerful concept is universally not leveraged by businesses today: The company's sales process only exists to fulfill the customer's purchase process. But what does the company call that touchpoint? Sales.

How are the supporting processes and infrastructure designed? They are designed to ideally execute a *sales* interaction.

From a customer's viewpoint, what is that same touchpoint interaction? It is—virtually without exception—seen as a *purchasing* (for commercial customers) or *buy* (for consumers) transaction.

How could a firm ideally provide value at that moment to generate incredible customer loyalty and return business? By designing the ideal purchase (not a sales) experience, a company's sales process could be an ideal input to and facilitator of the customer's purchasing process. In so doing, the company could potentially lower their customer's cost of the purchasing process, plus remove countless procedural hurdles to do business.

This same scenario—and opportunity to drive customer loyalty or defection—is applicable to all of the customer life-cycle touchpoints, but only if they are approached from a customer's point of view, not the company's culture.

In that customer-driven model:

- The company's sales process touchpoints are actually customer purchasing interactions and can be designed from that customer viewpoint.

- Company order fulfillment, shipping, and distribution actually facilitate customer receiving and can be designed to ideally access physical goods.

- Billing and accounts receivable interactions are actually accounts payable interactions from the customer view that can be designed to enable minimal administrative reconciliation and reduce payment costs.

- Post-sales service or maintenance interact with customer operations and can be designed to promote customer operational efficiency and minimal disruption.

Finally, customers should be segmented into groupings by the bank in order to receive segment-appropriate treatment, products, and services (one size does *not* fit all). However, the customer view of that segmentation is needs-based (see Figure 7.2) and not necessarily based on the products they happen to hold with that bank. In fact, a current product or service grouping is often insufficient to analyze and segment customers' needs. For example, a large group of current customers may have purchased fee-based investment advice elsewhere, but share the same needs as the customers who have acquired those products at the bank. If customers are segmented and treated based on their current products with the bank, the firm can miss this great opportunity for needs-based, targeted marketing.

No matter how well intentioned, a company's efforts to be customer friendly are often doomed to miss the mark. Unless they approach it from the customers' perspective and learn to integrate their two views, they remain vulnerable and the first new entry with a culture that lets customers actually design the relationship will **steal** the customers.

You Are the Customer

You are a customer.

If you are a commercial customer (a company), are your functional areas and processes that interact with your vendors complex? Costly? Time consuming?

What if a potential vendor engineered its culture and sales process to be the ideal interface to your purchasing process? What if everything you needed to locate, price out, and contract for materials, goods, and services was provided in an ideal manner to reduce the time, personnel, and costs you currently associate with buying supplies or replenishing inventory? If such a firm's products and prices were similar to others, might its touchpoints provide a value or benefit that could drive your loyalty and repeat business?

What if their prices were actually higher than their competitors? If you could make up with savings in your own processes, and then some, would you likely be a loyal, repeat customer? If someone other than your current vendor or supplier offered this benefit, might you move your business relationship to get it?

What other of your company's processes offers that type of opportunity to reduce costs, staffing, inventories, and so on?

If you are a consumer, can you envision similar benefits although your processes may be less formal or structured? If not savings in

consumer costs, what about savings in your time? Energy?
Anxiety?

- What about *your* customers? Are you losing customers,
  today? What about the future? What if someone else offers
  these types of benefits to your customers? Might a
  competitor with such a customer-focused culture and value
  proposition **steal** your customers?

- How easily could your customers defect? What would hold
  them loyal to you? What if your culture was more customer-
  oriented and your processes and touchpoints were
  relentlessly designed from your customers' perspectives to
  provide great value to them? Then how easily might they
  defect? How likely could someone **steal** them away?

- What if you offered those same benefits to your competitors'
  customers?

4

The Winning Customer Experience

I was a customer, and I wanted to buy bread.
"No, I cannot take your money. Fill out this form," you said.
"We have policies and processes and credit checks to do.
Then, if we find you qualify, we'll make some bread for you."
But all I wanted was to pay with cash, you see,
and hurry home with bread because a meal awaited me.
"That's not our business practice; you must obey our rules!
You customers are all the same, no respect for our schedules!"
I clenched the fist that held my cash, but then I looked away,
and saw a sign across the street: "Fresh Bread Sold—Your Way!"

— *Your former customer*

8

What They Want: Ten Myths About Your Customers

To become customer centered and customer preferred, a firm must change its orientation and design its business capabilities, infrastructure, and measures of success from the outside-in by using the customers' perspective. There are several real issues to overcome to do that. The first is that a firm's current beliefs about its customers tend to drive its policies, decision making, and not only what its employees do with customers, but also what they don't do. This becomes so embedded that firms practice this without realizing it, and it results in great resistance to new ideas about customers when the old ideas are so heavily ingrained.

The automobile company, for example, did not want to hear that customers were more interested in their coffee cup holders than other attributes of the vehicle. "We build cars for driving, not for drinking coffee" was a typical example of how a mindset about customers can filter out and resist hearing ideas or concepts that do not match prior conceptions about customers.

RETAIL BANK: LET'S ASK THE CUSTOMERS

At one of the largest, most successful banks in North America, I sat in the board room with a direct-report to the CEO and a group of other senior executives. They were in a quandary because tens of millions of dollars had been expended on telephone contact centers, yet the volume of calls was growing at such a rate that the capacity of that relatively new equipment would be exceeded in a year or so.

"Who's going to tell him?" asked one executive, referring to their CEO. No one made eye contact. Some examined the ceiling tiles, while other execs scrutinized their feet, apparently concerned that some shoelaces might be loose and in need of tying.

The silence grew heavy. Ultimately, as an outsider, I felt it was okay to fill the void and speak.

"I don't understand the problem," I said. "Didn't you say that if a customer comes into your bank it costs X to handle the interaction, but if they call your contact center it reduces your cost by 90 percent?"

RETAIL BANK: LET'S ASK THE CUSTOMERS (continued)

The executives looked back at me. One nodded in the affirmative.

"Then, isn't it a good thing that volumes are growing, because the more you can change customer behavior by providing a desirable, less-costly access channel, the more profit you will make? Don't you eventually want all customer contact to be conducted through low-cost channels, rather than via high-cost brick-and-mortar branches?"

Yes, they agreed, but they still had missed their forecast regarding when the current equipment would no longer handle the volume.

So I suggested that they come up with new reasons for volume to increase on the systems, such as things that weren't being done by the bank back at the time of the forecasts and when they bought the equipment. "Tie the equipment to initiatives that will add profit to the bank and that will be valid, positive reasons the equipment will need to be expanded. Make the additional capacity a good thing, linked to new, added revenue and not merely another unplanned expenditure."

"For example," I continued, "what about using the call center equipment for outbound calls to generate revenue? And what about doing cross-sell with the inbound customers who call you? Both of these would add additional volume and warrant expansion of the system, yet would be financially justified. In fact it would advance your current strategy to migrate customer interactions as much as possible to lower cost channels."

"Out of the question," said a senior manager.

"Why?" I asked.

RETAIL BANK: LET'S ASK THE CUSTOMERS (continued)

"Because customers hate to be called at home," he said, referring to my suggestion that their call center equipment be levered as a revenue generator, rather than simply to handle inbound service calls.

"And customers who have called in to us on a service topic don't want us trying to sell them something," offered another executive, referring to my suggestion of cross-sell during a customer service call.

"Always?" I asked, incredulously.

"Always," came the chorus.

And based upon that customer myth, a major firm had invested tens of millions in call center equipment, but only used it as an expense item, to handle inbound customer inquiries as inexpensively as possible. Their belief in their knowledge of what customers want and don't want had caused them not to lever the equipment for other revenue-generating uses—and to never question that decision.

"That is a hypothesis," I said, and then wrote their beliefs on the boardroom flipchart:

1. Customers do not want to be contacted by telephone. Always.

2. Customers do not want to receive another offer during a call they initiated. Always.

"Let's test these. Let's ask your customers," I challenged.

A few weeks later, the bank had a new set of customer-focused initiatives based on actual feedback from their customers. A customer vision had been developed, outside-in, of an ideal bank

RETAIL BANK: LET'S ASK THE CUSTOMERS (continued)

and of the ideal customer experiences during touchpoint interactions with such a bank's telephone contact center. The customer-defined vision caused such excitement that within a week it appeared on a plaque on the wall behind the desk of the CEO, who also directed that it be placed in the elevators of their headquarters. One element of that vision was the customers' view of how the bank could provide great benefit to them by contacting them at home (under certain circumstances, which the customers would highly value). Another was their vision of how an offer of a product during a service conversation (cross-sell) would not only be appropriate, but actually appreciated.

Securing an actionable, outside-in vision of your business from your customer can enable you to stay up with newly emerging needs and wants and to overcome the myths you currently have that impact your effectiveness. I have seen the above phenomenon many, many times. Think about the extent to which you may have similar mistaken beliefs about customers that are impacting your business.

What are your beliefs about your customers—what they want, what they don't want—that drive your business practices and product or process designs? Perhaps these were once valid, but have now changed. Why not ask the customer?

What do you argue about among yourselves as a management team? Is there one group or executive within your organization who believes your customers want/don't want something while another group or executive strongly disagrees? Why not ask the customer directly?

These are all things that beg market research, in order to overcome your mistaken or outdated beliefs. Although there is no substitute for research with your actual customers, to help you get started, we will next look at a few customer myths.

The Ten Common Myths

OUR CUSTOMERS:

1. Want the lowest price—period
2. *Other* key wants are known by us
3. Cannot envision what does not exist
4. Do not want to be telephoned at home—always
5. Do not want to be sold to when they call us
6. Do not want to provide us personal information
7. Hate to be transferred when they call
8. Won't accept an apology, so don't do it
9. Are unique, and so are their needs
10. Their needs (not wants) are known by us

Figure 8.1 Ten common myths about your customers.

Myth 1:
Our customers want the lowest price—period.

A powerful concept to remember is that your product or service offering is rarely a commodity that can only be differentiated by price. The fact is that the savvy business can differentiate even a roll of steel, arguably one of the most rock-solid examples of a commodity. The traditional way to compete with a commodity is to lower your cost of manufacturing, and then lower the price to drive additional sales and *"make it up on volume."*

Consider how to attract and retain customers on a value proposition other than price: What about their purchasing process? Their accounts payable process? The service they receive? The value-added expert advice that can be given to help the customer better use that product? In many cases these can be leveraged to provide great value to differentiate a firm or product and can often warrant your higher price, although your competitors offer a lower price.

Myth 2:
We know what our customers want (or don't want).

Perhaps the greatest inhibitor to go beyond "Have a nice day" service platitudes is the belief within a firm that its prior history and years of experience result in perfect knowledge of what customers want and do not want. Virtually every firm at one time has felt it could skip the development of requirements via "customer visioning" and go straight to implementation of new processes and channels for customers. After all, the firm has been in that business for (insert number of decades here) and no one knows their customers better than they do.

There is, in fact, someone else who better knows what the customer wants—the customer! In order to develop an ideal, customer-defined future vision of the firm, there is no other substitute.

That does not mean that the company has no valuable information at all. Front-line, customer-facing personnel can be a valuable source of information regarding the *performance* of current processes, channels, and product or service offerings. Customer complaints and customer service contacts provide excellent feedback on what's not working. The important thing in those cases, however, is that the information still come directly from the customer, not from your intuition due to years of "being in the business."

However, over time it can become less clear which of your beliefs regarding customers is actual, literal customer feedback versus intuitive beliefs formed and reformed over the years. The result can be a strongly held set of beliefs, such as those of the bank contact center, that are rigidly driving the wrong actions. Even if you once knew exactly what your customers wanted, in the current environment of rapidly rising service levels, those desires are fast-changing and if you have no formal vehicles to monitor these, then you do not know them.

Finally, while front-line employees may know what customers like or dislike about current products and services, they often lack the ability to place themselves in the customer's position to envision creative new offerings and interactions that would appeal to deeply hidden or newly emerging customer value systems. By probing directly with the customers why they want things—and understanding how customers get value/benefit from the things they want—it is possible to jointly envision and develop creative, new breakthrough ideas. Which brings us to the next customer myth.

Myth 3:
Customers cannot envision what does not exist; focus groups are a waste of money and, besides, no Sony customer ever envisioned the WalkMan.

This wonderful myth is born from many firms expending great sums on research, and sitting for hours behind one-way mirrors watching ineffective focus groups that yield little of value. Anything, done the wrong way, can be disappointing and ineffective, including focus groups.

It may be true that engineers, not customers, envisioned the Sony WalkMan. Probably no customer spontaneously said, "Eureka, I want to take my big console radio and strap it to my head for music while I am out jogging—if only engineers could reduce the size of the components and then come up with cool-looking headphones."

But that is not because customers lack the capability to envision things that do not exist. Rather, it is because market research techniques often do not generate a line of thinking that breaks the person out of using only currently available and existing things to develop their vision.[1]

With such approaches, Sony could have arrived at the same idea, probably earlier, and from a customer. And with such approaches, so can you.

Myth 4:
Customers do not want to be telephoned at home—always.

As the banking client learned, it is unwise to project your own personal prejudices, likes, and dislikes onto your customers. The bankers were far off the mark and did not understand what their customers truly wanted. When we asked the executives if they based their beliefs on actual customer input, their answer was, "Sure. We all have a wife or husband who is a customer."

Beyond the obvious issue of the statistical validity of a sample size of a half-dozen spouses, these bankers clearly had not read the chapter on segmentation to know that what one customer hates, another may actually like—or read the previous Myth 3 on how

---

1. At IBM, we developed approaches that helped a customer to go beyond the "what" that they wanted and focus on "why" and how they would receive value and benefit from it. A vision could then be developed of different, ideal delivery of that value or benefit (the why, not the what) unconstrained by currently existing products, processes, or technologies.

customers can methodically be led to develop a vision of how they might receive ideal value during an interaction. If the bankers had read these things, they might have tested their hypothesis themselves—with customers.

In fact, customers in visioning workshops for many different industries have stated that the primary problem with being contacted at home is that it is almost always by a blanket marketing program and not targeted to their specific interests. Customers hate to be contacted when the call has nothing uniquely to do with them, but is merely part of a mass-marketing campaign: "Don't call me about your great special on boat insurance if I don't own a boat!"

However, if a customer owns a particular investment product and something happens that could impact them personally—perhaps new legislation that could have tax implications—they would actually appreciate receiving a targeted, personalized, individual-specific contact. "Except during the dinner hour. Always."

Myth 5:
Customers do not want to be sold to when they telephone for service.

This is a common misconception resulting in missed opportunities in all industries to provide great customer value during touch-point interactions.

As with all these items, there is both opportunity and risk involved. The risk with this one is twofold: First, never try to sell a customer something until you have handled—to *their* satisfaction—whatever the issue was for which they originally called. Second, never make a generalized, mass-market, blanket offer. The opportunity here is reciprocal: After the customer's issue has been addressed, it is almost always appropriate to make them an offer as long as it is tailored and targeted to their personal interests and values. "Mr. Thompson, I'm glad we could resolve that for you. Before we end our discussion, I see that you are an avid golfer (perhaps Thompson used his credit card to charge a set of clubs or a golf cart rental). As you may know, our travel service department has a special offer for two nights at the Hilton in Myrtle Beach, with free golf, for only $99.00 next weekend. Would you be interested?"

Myth 6:
Customers do not want to give us information about themselves.

In today's world there are well-publicized and growing public concerns regarding the use of personal information. These include, but are certainly not limited to, real issues of invasion of privacy, breach of confidentiality, identity theft, and plain old irritation at being contacted by someone who has obtained one's phone number, postal address, or Internet address.

However, customers also place a high value on the benefits and value they can receive (see Myths 4 and 5 above) from targeted, individualized, and customer-specific interactions. For example, the term *tailored and personalized* crept into their vocabulary by the late 1990s. During the early 2000s, personalization moved from a distant rumble of occasional customer delight to a roar of expectations. And to receive the benefits of targeted, personalized products and services customers must now enable their vendor with relevant data about themselves. In return, the firm must secure the data (with controlled, employee-only, and role-appropriate access) and then use it only for the purposes for which it was provided. With these assurances, and some well-earned trust in your brand, customers will share information with you. This is a highly volatile and critical issue that represents both opportunity and risk to the extreme. Personalized interactions can literally become your most powerful loyalty generator, but if you misuse customer information and lose their trust, you can lose not only your customers, but also your market.

Myth 7:
Customers who call hate to be transferred.

While this statement appears to be intuitively correct, the reality is actually counter-intuitive and it depends on why they are calling. If a customer contacts your firm for general information regarding your business, products, prices, and so on, they may well expect to get an answer from their first point of contact. However, if they want expert advice, they do not expect the first person who answers incoming calls to also be an expert in all things. In this case, a transfer of their call can actually reassure them they are going to the "right" person who has the expertise. However, that should occur with no more than one transfer.

Myth 8:
An apology is never enough (so we don't do it).

A common myth that drives the behavior of customer-facing employees is: Our customers don't want an apology; they only want some form of personal compensation or concession for mistakes. In many businesses that myth is not only accepted, culturally, but it is an actual business practice to never admit or take responsibility, for fear it would only encourage the customer to feel aggrieved and would somehow later be held against them.

This is almost universally incorrect. In fact, customers repeatedly say that the most powerful thing a firm can do after an error is to admit it—and apologize. However, in order to have the greatest effect, the apology should also be accompanied by assurance that action has been taken to insure the error will not occur again. For example, an apology during the customer interaction, followed by a letter from management that the reason for the mistake has been determined and that corrective measures are now in place, can actually increase loyalty. Customers are often delighted with how a firm responds to and corrects a mistake. Customer defections in those instances were actually less than the defection rate of customers who had experienced no problems at all.

Myth 9:
Our customers and their needs are unique.

Another common misconception is that customer needs for a given firm, industry, or geography are unique and quite different from those of other firms, industries, or geographies.

Virtually everyone needs responsive service, and easy, timely access to their vendors, irrespective of industry.[2] However, the customers of a stock brokerage will place a higher priority on quick and easy access to placing their orders than customers of a locomotive manufacturer. The customers of an accountant will more greatly demand precision than customers of a hair stylist, although it is a need shared by both.

Within an industry, customer segments will tend to have similar needs but different priorities, e.g., financial services where older people value safety over growth and younger ones tend to prefer taking risks in order to attain growth. Both groups need growth and safety, but to attract and retain each of them requires a dramatically different offering by the industry.

Beyond the prioritization or importance weighting differences, we also find that approximately 30 percent or so of the actual customer needs are often unique to a specific industry or customer set. What is important here is:

· A firm can begin its customer journey and focus on some basic needs that are relatively common to all customers (and which I will share with you in the next chapter).

---

2. When IBM established a global consulting business to help clients become customer centered, we also expected great differences in customer needs among the industries. To be sure, we found many differences, and some were critical to survival within a given industry or unique to a specific customer segment. But a powerful finding was that approximately 70 percent (my estimate) of the expressed needs from almost all customers were quite similar. What differed were their priorities.

- Once the firm can "walk" and provide such basic loyalty-driving needs, it can progress to "run," via market research to determine the 30 percent or so of unique needs and any prioritization differences that may be necessary to attract and retain segments.

- However, it is dangerous to then assume that when a business model is successful for one customer set that it can be cloned as "our standard set of corporate processes" and will work around the world. It's that 30 percent of variability that can still kill the business.

GLOBAL FINANCIAL SERVICES: THEY LOVE IT IN SYDNEY

The VP of business process engineering for a firm in Australia was deservedly proud of the standardized business processes that had been established across their Aussie locations. As a result, he said not only had costs been brought under control, but market share had improved. As we talked, however, he expressed frustration with a new venture they had recently started in Ireland. It seemed that the acquired firm's employees strongly resisted many of the standard processes, and customers were complaining and/or leaving.

What the company had failed to recognize was the 30 percent factor, and that the key wants and needs or priorities of their customers in Australia would not be the same as in Ireland.

Myth 10:
We know what our customers need
(not want . . . *need*).

This myth or misunderstanding is tightly linked to our earlier discussions that firms founded on their own internal expertise and product knowledge often continue to believe that, due to their product expertise, they are the experts on what customers *need*. This is quite different from the issue of what customers *want*. It assumes that product expertise equates to also knowing what is best for the customer. In fact, firms with extreme product competence may be even less likely than others to know the (changing) needs of their customers. These firms are also the ones less likely to have processes and competencies for listening, understanding, and responding to customers in a rapidly changing environment.

Beyond that, even the companies that listen to what customers want almost always lack the insight required to know and fully leverage what the customer actually *needs* and would most value. This is because only the customer completely understands how they get value or benefit from something they want, and that underlying benefit is *why they NEED it*. Understanding *what* they want is good. Understanding *why* they need it is critical to creatively develop new products and services to better meet those needs. And that is why the customers, not only the company, must be included in creative visioning of needs-based, future products and services (see Chapter 9, "What They Need: Customer Visioneering").

You Are the Customer

What about when you are the customer?

Do you always search out the lowest price? And do you always then purchase from that low-cost provider? Always?

If not, when have you bought something and known a similar item was available elsewhere and cheaper? Why? What was it that you valued greater than price?

Have you ever been contacted by phone, at home, and actually appreciated the call? Why? What was it that you valued greater than being undisturbed?

Have you ever received an offer or proposal, although you originally initiated the contact on a different subject, and appreciated it? Why? What makes it okay in your mind, even great, to be offered something (such as a product or service)?

When you contact a business, do you expect the first person that answers the phone to be able to answer questions or handle issues on any topic? Why or why not?

If you need advice on a complex matter such as investment products, do you expect to be transferred to reach an expert on that subject? If you were not transferred to someone who specialized in such a topic, would you be comfortable with and trust the answers you get?

Do you think the above is true only for financial issues, advice, and counsel? Or is it also true for other businesses—such as yours? For example, how secure are you that a salesperson can also give you accurate technical advice about the electronics under the hood of your new ZOT 12? Would you be happy if a single transfer could get you from the salesperson to the right technically knowledgeable person?

What if a business made a major mistake with your account? Would it be important to you that they apologized? What if they did not? What if they would not even admit to the error?

Can a vendor best envision new products or services to meet your *unexpressed future needs*, or would you need to apply your knowledge of *why* you need things and *how* you could get the greatest benefit or value? For example, can you envision teaming with a vendor and discussing why you want what you want and then together envisioning new ways they could better provide that benefit?

Could a firm that offers this **steal** away your business?

- What about *your* customers?
- Would they answer the above very differently?
- Are you treating them differently?

9

What They Need: Customer Visioneering

ustomer wants and needs is a common phrase that is often heard and seldom understood. Most folks don't know the difference. However, the winners do and if you want your firm to be a winner, then so must you. Because the difference is:

- A customer "want" is something they expressly state as a desired outcome.

- A customer "need" is the underlying value or benefit that drives their "wants."

Here is an example: Athletes often *want* a cold beverage to quench their thirst. However, the underlying *need* is because they sweat to maintain a safe temperature and then must rehydrate to replenish lost liquids, vital electrolytes, and carbohydrates. For years, the beverage industry focused solely on the want: a thirst quencher. Then the University of Florida focused on the underlying need, which (not coincidentally) also enabled greater athletic stamina and performance. Based on that needs-based value proposition, an entire industry for sports drinks has since been developed, including the pioneer Gatorade.

Here's another example: Business people often *want* a rental car, but the rental car firm is not actually in the business of fulfilling customer needs for a rental car. Their customers *want* a rental car, but what they *need* is to get to and/or from an airport, train station, hotel, business site, home, and so on. So rental car firms are actually in the human logistics (or the "get me there efficiently, effectively, and alive") business. As such, their competitors are not limited to rental car companies, nor is their optimum value proposition (ideal fulfillment of the needs) limited to providing a rental vehicle. If you ask your customers why they need a given product, touchpoint, or channel, you can then have them envision the ideal means to fulfill that need—and new ways *to keep your customers* (or **steal** new ones).

TRAVEL: IDEALLY FULFILLING A NEED

I once did that with a group of business travelers to test the concept. They envisioned the ideal means to travel to a remote business location or meeting. A single step could reserve and coordinate multi-vendor capabilities that today require customers to engage several firms—each of whom believe they are in the taxi, airline, rental car, or hotel fulfillment business. It was a door-to-door vision based on their underlying *needs* ("Get me from here to my meeting, alive and on time.") rather than the more commonly expressed *wants* regarding the individual piece-parts such as taxis, airplanes, rental cars, or hotels.

For example, a sole transaction would secure transport from home or office to the airport and insure just-in-time arrival at the departure gate, ticketed and pre-checked-in. Later, their vision was to deplane and proceed directly through the airport terminal to the curbside where a car would await (professional driver optional) *with their baggage already in the vehicle's luggage compartment.* Cross-enterprise processes and capabilities would be orchestrated and coordinated as a single performance between ground transportation, air carriers, hotels, and/or business meeting facilities and would ultimately generate a single "business trip" invoice.

While you may feel this is impractical, consider the competitive edge that firms in such a multi-company value chain would have if their services were focused and coordinated to seamlessly deliver the overriding customer *need* rather than a piece-part *want*.

Opportunities are practically endless to go beyond what customers say they want and envision ideal delivery of their underlying needs. As Jan Carlsen said years ago, "There are thousands (he was wrong; for a sizable business there are millions) of moments of truth each day with customers." Those touchpoints offer your business the opportunity to determine customers' needs at each critical moment and find ways for creative, breakthrough delivery.

Okay, you may be thinking, but give me a more realistic, practical example, not some big pie-in-the-sky, multi-company deal. Years ago, customers complained that they wanted shorter waiting lines (queues) at their banks and much longer banking hours. But the underlying value of shorter lines and longer banking hours was that they *needed* quick and easy access to their cash or information regarding their account. When complaints reached a high level, banks would traditionally scurry around and literally cut up short lengths of rope to create more, and shorter, waiting lines. Employees would be asked to work different shifts in order to keep the bank open and available to customers more hours and days each week.

Ultimately, someone thought to address the "why" (*quick and easy access to my cash and information about my account*) rather than the "what" they wanted. A technological solution of automated teller machines (ATMs) was found to be the ideal solution at the time, providing breakthrough delivery. Later, of course, telephone banking and, more recently, Internet transactions have provided new ways to fill those needs. The point is that no one came in and asked for "a mechanical robot to replace your human tellers," just as no customers had likely asked Sony for a way to strap a console radio on their heads (the WalkMan). But a major break-through in value delivery occurred when the first bank went beyond what the customer *wanted* and developed an ideal delivery of why they *needed* it.

As another example, grocery stores often added checkout lanes and additional staff because that is what their customers wanted. Why customers *needed* that, however, was for faster egress from the store with their purchases. Breakthrough delivery of that need was accomplished via bar code scanners, which at the time were being used to read labels on the side of boxcars, not cereal boxes, for inventory control in rail yards. As a result, better inventory control was also experienced by the grocery stores, as well as improved customer throughput and lower costs.

This is reverse engineering when you look backward from such early customer-focused breakthroughs, and you can see how to re-create the same "quantum leap" effect today through use of outside-in, customer thinking to envision new offerings and touchpoint capabilities.

This difference between a customer *want* and a customer *need* is extremely powerful and offers a place to stand and envision, then develop the greatest possible customer value at key touchpoint interactions. You know the phrase by Archimedes, "Give me a platform on which to stand and a long enough lever and I can move the world." Identifying customers' needs provides you with that platform and a powerful lever to attract or **steal** additional market share, as well as *keep your customers in an era of easy defection.*

The problem is that most firms not only believe they know what customers want, they also believe they know what customers need—ad nauseum. As a result, businesses often feel over-whelmed and unable to economically fulfill what seems like endless wish lists of customer desires. Management is often distracted by (and scarce resources are unevenly spread across) an undisciplined set of customer issues, rather than focused on a short list of needs that drive loyalty (see Figure 9.1).

Figure 9.1 No wish lists allowed! Isolate the loyalty drivers and discard the rest.

The powerful concept in Figure 9.1 can have a major impact on your business. Companies today commonly expend their resources on well-intentioned, but *ineffective* initiatives to provide their customers' identified wants and needs. Why? Because *the bulk of customers' expressed wants and needs do not drive their buying behavior or loyalty,* and firms fail to isolate and focus on the critical few that do.

Imagine that you have taken your customers' (non-price-related) known needs and wants and placed them in a horizontal array. At each end, left and right, you separate out the ones that drive the most extreme behavior, i.e., the critical few that drive defection if not received are on the left side and those that would attract a customer away if available elsewhere are on the right side. If the remainder were placed in the center, they would greatly outnumber the critical few at the extreme ends, which drive negative and positive behavior. You would also have constructed a bell-shaped curve, with the outliers representing the most powerful levers to influence your customers with things they value other than price.

Those three groupings of needs/wants would then offer you a rational means of prioritizing areas of focus and investment for your firm, as well as areas in which to disinvest:

1. The highest priority must be directed to the short list stacked on the left. In this era of *easy defection*, you must deliver those or your customers will leave.

2. After the "must haves" above, the second-highest priority goes to the short list stacked on the right, which provide things that could differentiate your firm, attract new customers, and gain (**steal**) market share from competitors.

3. The third priority group—middle of the curve and potentially the largest number of known customer needs and wants—should literally be discarded from your investments, management focus, business practices, and metrics of success. Individually, they have little or no impact on customer buying behavior. They represent the background noise from your customers that daily distracts management attention and wastes critical resources. (The exception might be when several of these, done collectively, could have a positive, cost-effective impact on your image.)

There are market research firms and consulting firms that can help you to structure and execute research to build such a model with your specific customers. Companies often resist doing that because they believe they already know their customers' wants and needs or because they feel it is too costly. But, this can actually be one of the most cost-effective expenditures (investments) that your company can make: It not only tells you what to do to *keep your customers*, but also tells you what you do not have to do. In a world of undisciplined customer requirements—where they have an unlimited ability to ask, but you have limited capabilities to respond—identifying what *you do not have to do* is incredibly valuable.

Earlier chapters discussed why structured research with customers is critical: Customers tend to cluster into needs-based groups (segments) and you will need specific, possibly different, infrastructure and capabilities to attract and keep each group. To effectively do so, you must secure your customers' visions and insights on not only what they want, but why (the need) and the ideal delivery of that need.

Experience has revealed a pattern of repeating wants and needs that seem to cover nearly 70 percent of what customers express. Your customers will have their own segment-specific priorities, and potentially 30 percent or more of unique wants and needs. As you progress from walk to run on this path, you will ultimately need professional researchers and consultants to understand those unique needs and priorities of your actual customers.

Interim to such research, here is a starter set of *walk before you run*, commonly expressed wants and/or needs. Within these are items that for some of your customers are absolute "must-haves," and would drive their defection if not provided. Other items, for some customer segments, will be "attractors" that would not cause them to leave if not provided, but would powerfully differentiate a competitor and attract those customers away if available elsewhere.

First, let's look at some of the commonly expressed, but quite important, "must-have" behavior drivers from the left side of the bell curve (see Figure 9.2).

It's easy to believe that the most powerful negative drivers of customer behavior and attrition are intuitively obvious and therefore not an issue, i.e., lack of courtesy or lack of competence. Still, these remain the most often cited reasons for customers to actually leave and not return. Although they may seem self-evident to you, we should begin with an examination of these two from a customer perspective.

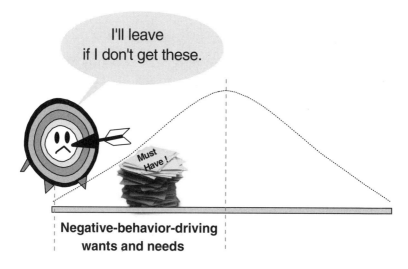

#1 Priority: Deliver "Must-Haves"!

Figure 9.2 *Who stole my customer??* (negative levers).

Lack of Courtesy: First Among the Major Drivers of Defection

What do customers want or need regarding courtesy? What are the attributes of courtesy that customers use to assess a firm? Customers now define their expectations for courtesy to be much more than merely the absence of rudeness. Courtesy is expected to be a highly visible manifestation of an overarching mind-set within a firm to be customer focused and to help solve the customer's issue. Further, the firm must consistently demonstrate an enterprise-wide, customer-focused culture.

How do customers know it when they see it? Courtesy is not limited to a pleasant reaction to a customer's inquiry, request, or complaint; it is most effective and evident when practiced proactively.

OFFICE SUPPLY: COURTESY? WE'VE GOT THAT

Recently, I went into a Staples office supply store in Danbury, CT. I was browsing their shelves to see if they had a solution to a home-office decorating problem. I did not know exactly what I needed, and my face probably reflected some confusion as I walked the aisles.

During the ensuing 20 minutes or so, I was approached by no fewer than five non-management employees who asked if I needed assistance. These were not salespeople motivated by commissions from my purchases. All were doing some form of manual labor, and they interrupted their tasks to try to help me. One was straightening merchandise on a shelf, and when she saw me looking at nearby items, she stopped her work and said, "Let me get out of your way so you can also see these." Then, "Is there anything I can help with?" On another aisle, two young men were working as a team to move heavy boxes of printer paper up a ladder for storage atop the shelving. One stopped their process to inquire—from the ladder—if I was, "finding everything okay?"

This happened several more times, until I actually did have a need for help. I then stopped a person who happened to walk nearby and inquired if a package might be reduced in price because it had been opened. Someone had removed part of the materials, and it was the

OFFICE SUPPLY: COURTESY? WE'VE GOT THAT (continued)

only one left on the shelf. The clerk disappeared for a few minutes and then returned with a discounted price, hand-written on the package, which she took to the cashier and explained the exception.

All of this occurred an hour before the Super Bowl (U.S. National Football League championship game) was scheduled to begin that evening on television. On a day that many people did not wish to work, rather than a sullen "why us" attitude, I experienced proactive courtesy. And there was no doubt in my mind as to whether these were isolated anomalies. This was clear, anecdotal evidence of a customer-focused culture. More importantly, I got their message: *Our culture is enterprise-wide—not just limited to a functional area such as sales or service—and you can expect to get such treatment, on time, every time.*

The definition of courtesy in the minds of customers today is that it evidences a proactive, cross-functional, enterprise-wide culture, right? Yes. And more.

When the ideal delivery of courtesy is described, customers repeatedly use the word "empathy." The employee who approaches a topic with an awareness of how the customer feels, then relates to that and "takes the customer side" best exemplifies courtesy. It goes beyond friendliness to actual helpfulness and a focus on finding a resolution to the customer's problem, i.e., caring is another commonly heard term.

Chapter 9
What They Need: Customer Visioneering

To re-emphasize an earlier point: An apology can be seen as the most sincere form of a customer focus and courtesy. Employees should apologize for errors made by their firm. To have the most impact, and to demonstrate that the company is going beyond mere platitudes, the apology must be personalized by clearly recognizing what happed to that individual customer, ideally coupled with what the firm is doing to prevent root-cause recurrence to any customer.

What can your firm do for even higher levels of customer loyalty impact? Often, a major lever (*in an era of easy defection*) is to exceed proactive courtesy with an even stronger demonstration that you "value" a customer. There are segments that appreciate experiences such as the one at Staples, where it is clear that all customers are highly valued. However, many people are in segments that respond most favorably when the specific value of that customer to the firm is apparent in their treatment. An example is the special treatment received by whole classes of customers of airlines and hotels who enjoy *bronze, silver, or gold* status, consistent with their value to the company. Providing that on an individualized basis, rather than by segment membership, is an even better way to demonstrate a customer-focused culture, although significantly harder and more costly to implement (see "The Ultimate Want: Tailored and Personalized Offerings" on page 141 of this chapter).

The need for a consistent, enterprise-wide culture of relentless customer focus is a point oft repeated. While this can be extremely difficult to establish across a sizable organization or brand (and can warrant a book on that topic, alone), perhaps the greater exposure lies outside the company. Business partners, outsourced functions, and other third parties often have direct contact with your customers that reflects on your firm and impacts loyalty and attrition. Outsourced customer contact centers, for example, have become quite common and have obvious financial benefits. The downside can be far less obvious, as third-party staffs interact with your customers but lack the training, espirit des corps, and motivation of your own employees, or the customer focus promised by your brand. Without an investment on your part to insure all customer contact points have access to the same customer information, for example, a consistent customer experience is greatly at risk.

Competence: Typically Second Among Drivers of Defection

Beyond a positive, customer-focused, courteous attitude, what do customers want or need regarding the actual competency of a vendor? What are the key attributes of competence that customers use to assess a firm? While an absence of precision or accuracy can be a major indicator of incompetence, the presence of accuracy and precision certainly does not complete the customers' vision of a competent vendor.

Much like courtesy, competence is not the absence of something, such as errors. Rather, it is evidenced by the proactive presence of many things and in a manner to suggest enterprise-wide institutionalization.

Chapter 9
What They Need: Customer Visioneering

Precise and error-free execution of complex skills are attributes of competence. However, the obvious presence of proactive measures to prevent errors, or to quickly and actively correct them, can have even greater impact on customer perceptions and increase their trust in your competence. A few years back a bank in the U.S. tried to exploit that phenomenon by placing an error on customers' statements, then contacting them to say, "We found an error, and we corrected it." The ploy backfired when customers learned of this shameful manipulation. Which brings us to another attribute of customer-perceived competence: image and reputation.

A firm's (or brand's) image can be a primary means to manage customer perception regarding competence. This is an example where virtually all customers have the same wants or needs, but the weighting and importance can vary greatly based on the customer segment or your industry. Customers of the financial services industry, airlines, or surgical clinics will place a far greater emphasis on accuracy and precision, supported by the firm's/brand's image as well as personal experience, than customers of other less critical industries. Whatever the industry, the important factor is that the image be in synch with the firm's actual capabilities to perform. One of the fastest routes to lost customers is to raise customer expectations via promises made in advertising and then underperform.

Other key attributes of competence include not only being skilled but also empowered to act. That is because competence is best demonstrated by results. No matter how skilled (and courteous) your employee might be, if they are powerless to act and attain the desired result then customers view your touchpoint contact as incompetent. The smart firm empowers customer-facing personnel by providing them a range of authority to make on-the-spot decisions or concessions. By setting the range (such as *up to $50* and so on) a company can limit its financial exposure and reduce the cost of unnecessary management escalations, yet provide customers with a more positive experience.

The term "empowerment" is greatly overused and often highly resented by employees. That is because their empowerment means very little without some accompanying enablement, which management often ignores. Changes must also be made to infrastructure to give the employees the additional capabilities and information they will need. If employees are empowered to make customer concessions based on the value or past history of a customer, then they will need the real-time capability and infrastructure to access such data. Often, the employee is actually placed in an untenable situation and the result is that customers are then told of the back-office horrors that constrict the employee. One of my early client-engagement reports, for example, included a chart that was headed "Good people, poor processes." The bad news: it was the client's customers who told me this, because the employees had told them. The client's financial services brand image for competence had been seriously undermined.

Competence is further demonstrated by the consistent ability to meet your commitments (do what you say) or to take responsibility to secure a correct outcome when things go wrong. Transferring a customer to someone who has the ability to secure the final action is good; however, it is even better when the first person contacted takes ownership of the issue and stays involved until final resolution.

Loyal customers from the top competitor to a major firm in the Midwest United States once stated that no matter who was called at the competitive firm, that person took responsibility for resolution of virtually any issue the customer raised, irrespective of the topic or their functional area. The customers greatly valued dealing with a single firm rather than individual departments and said such attributes were why they would likely not leave or *defect* from this popular competitor. In fact, some had actually *defected* from other vendors and were attracted to and **stolen** by this competitor due to a reputation for that form of competency (as the customers defined it).

The actual customer view of such needs and wants is not always as intuitive or obvious as you might think. Following is a continued list of commonly heard needs and wants and their customer-defined attributes.

A Rising Expectation: Knowledgeable Point of Contact

What do customers expect regarding a knowledgeable representative at your firm? Over the past five years that has changed dramatically. The obvious answer is that customers expect your contact personnel to be knowledgeable about your own products.

This has historically included current inventory availability, future manufacturing, or delivery schedules and prices. As your products become more complex, such as information technology, the level of knowledge customers expect expands to also include configuration assistance regarding combinations of those products or features that work well together. In other words, from what they *want* (the product) to why they *need* it (the potential result of the product). In today's world, with firms' increased efforts to differentiate themselves via service, this has expanded to often include expecting expert "integration" knowledge of your competitors' products and mixed-vendor configurations.

In fact, the definition of a knowledgeable contact person at your firm is now typically someone who (in the customer's words):

- Knows all the available products and services
  - knows your firm's offerings
  - knows your competitors' offerings

- Understands my needs and wants
  - understands me
  - understands my industry (commercial customer)
  - understands my company (commercial customer)

- Proposes the best match of available products to my needs
  - knows best match of products and my capabilities to use them
  - knows solutions to improve my business (commercial customer)

- Can educate and/or advise me on the use of products

Chapter 9
What They Need: Customer Visioneering

In this scenario, firms must realize that they are no longer in business to sell products (what customers want) but rather they must now provide solutions (what customers need). Major firms, such as IBM and virtually all the technology giants, are institutionalizing this by transforming their business strategy and infrastructure to be both service- and solutions-focused, not product-focused (see "The Ultimate Need: A Solution—Not a Product, Not a Service" on page 149 of this chapter).

Because complex, specialized knowledge is often required to provide such solutions, customers do not expect the first point of contact, or whoever answers the phone, to coincidentally have such knowledge. In a complex solutions scenario, requiring specialized skills, it may not be practical for the first point of contact to take ownership through to actual resolution (as with the Midwest firm in the prior example). Customers do, however, expect your people to understand your own internal organization and to take ownership to find the appropriately knowledgeable person. Do not make the customer navigate your internal organization structure to find the knowledge or capabilities match for his or her issue. The first person to take a customer's call, no matter how far afield their role may be from the customer issue, should take responsibility to connect the customer with the appropriate party.

While this is often difficult within large companies, it is critical. When customers approach a business today via multiple channels and/or business units, the challenge to the firm is to enable each of those disparate contact points to provide a consistent, information-enabled experience. Businesses around the world are working hard to develop the infrastructure to provide such an experience. A larger issue can be for this to extend beyond the company to its business partners and franchisees. An equally important, but less focused upon, area is that of their outsourced contact points.

OUTSOURCED TELEPHONE CONTACT CENTER: *1-800-WHO-CARES*

As a WorldCom customer, I received a series of erroneous monthly telephone invoices. I contacted them regarding the errors, only to see those repeated or worse in the following months. Ultimately, the bills began to arrive with an accompanying message that they were in error and to disregard them. This was confusing, because if they knew this then why did they mail them? About that time, I began to hear national news reports of widespread customer complaints. Then I began to receive telephone calls demanding my immediate payment of the same invoices that I had been told to not pay.

I asked their representative why they were calling to collect invoices that:

    a. WorldCom knew to be in error

    b. I had contacted WorldCom to discuss, repeatedly

    c. I had been told to disregard

The response was that the customer contact person was unaware of the company's billing problems and did not know their invoices had a note accompanying them. He also did not know I had spoken

**OUTSOURCED TELEPHONE CONTACT CENTER: *1-800-WHO-CARES*
(continued)**

repeatedly with WorldCom customer service about my account. So,
I then spoke with a supervisor and requested that she please inform
her WorldCom management that the left hand (billing process) did
not know what the right hand (customer service and collections) was
doing. At that point she admitted that she had no direct interaction
with WorldCom and no idea how to send them such customer
feedback. She was an employee of a third-party, outsourced,
customer contact firm and had no direct knowledge of what was
occurring within the company. As far as I was concerned, however,
WorldCom had a big problem and a very dissatisfied customer on a
topic that impacted my loyalty.

A Simple-Sounding Expectation: Responsiveness

Customers have always expected a responsive touchpoint experience. But what does that mean today? This item has become
increasingly complex as rapid changes in the marketplace also
tend to reset customer expectations at a similar, fast rate.

If asked, "What do your customers want regarding responsiveness?" a typical business person must now respond, "You mean
yesterday? Or today?"

Here are three major topics that currently relate to customers'
expectations for responsiveness:

- Responsive attitudes

- Responsive/timely actions

- Responsive offerings

First, a responsive attitude is the front-of-mind implication of the term; it goes far beyond customer-first slogans and is highly action oriented. A can-do, I'll-handle-it attitude is more than ever the benchmark for responsiveness, rather than mere turnaround time, which is also important and follows next. Customers characterize a responsive attitude with phrases such as "service oriented" and "helpful." This hallmark of responsiveness has to do with the company's willingness to adapt to the needs of the customer. The days of citing company rules and procedures, or hiding behind statements of corporate policy, are no longer accepted in lieu of customer-focused action as a firm's response. The visible presence of exception processes to handle non-standard or emergency customer situations provides a reassuring image of such a responsive vendor.

Second, responsiveness is seen in the timing and handling of actions by the company. This means not only quick turnaround time to a request, but also being agile and able to react to changes in an individual customer's requirements or in the marketplace as a whole. In fact, the ability to sense changes in the marketplace and respond is perhaps the most critical capability common to most industries today. Such companies maintain lead times that are kept in alignment with the changing needs of the marketplace, plus the flexibility to adapt to an individual customer's non-standard needs.

Third, responsiveness can be seen in the products (and design of touchpoints) of a company. The responsive firm senses market needs and responds with appropriate products, services, access channels, and customer-facing processes. Inventories reflect a knowledge of and alignment with market needs. Choices are offered, and the contents of those are customer defined, because all customers do not want the same things. Customers are treated as the experts whose opinions drive product development and user requirements.

A major exposure to a firm's, or brand's, public perception and image can also be other downstream organizations. Just as customer perception of your firm's courtesy, competence, or knowledge can be impacted by business partners, franchisees, and outsourced activities, the *responsiveness* of those units can also be attributed to you. MasterCard and American Express provide excellent examples.

While American Express has a great deal of customer contact under its direct control, other services such as financial planning by AMEX Financial Advisors are often provided by franchisee professional planners, who are not actual AMEX employees. These planners operate under the umbrella of the American Express Financial Advisors logo, and AMEX is well aware that the activities of such extended enterprise parties reflect directly on the public's perception of the brand. As a result, high performance standards and safeguards are in place to protect the brand.

Responsiveness at MasterCard or Visa can be an even more difficult issue. In their cases, most customers with credit cards see their logo and toll-free telephone numbers for customer service and are unaware the contact center is staffed by the issuing bank or a third-party provider. From the customers' perspective, they are calling MasterCard, not Acme Bank, and any lack of responsiveness is perceived as a brand issue. Even in the minds of customers who realize they are speaking with a bank or out-sourced center, the brand remains responsible for the performance of its surrogates.

The irony here is that the banks collectively own and control Mas-terCard, which is an entity formed by and for the banks. From a brand standpoint, the card's image is impacted by the best and the worst performers among thousands of banks that actually own the brand. So, how does the card enforce a common standard of performance across thousands of organizations that actually own the brand? Their solution: customers were seg-mented and targeted based on their wants, needs, and value to the brand. Then the customers were asked to set the standards for responsiveness and other wants and needs, which the brand could then use to promote a more consistent customer experi-ence across all the member banks, business partners, and out-sourced functions. If you have third parties that interface with your customers, perhaps a similar approach is in order. Have your customers define the performance standards, and then have cus-tomers appraise the organizations against those standards.

The Ultimate Want: Tailored and Personalized Offerings

Of course, the customers' ultimate vision of an ideally responsive firm leads us to the subject of tailored, personalized service. The preceding customer wants or needs were primarily discussed as drivers of negative behavior if not provided (*I'll leave if I don't get these!*), although there will be some segments of your customers who would not leave over those. Similarly, there are also expressed wants and needs that offer such positive value that some segments would be *attracted or* stolen *away from current vendors* if available elsewhere (see Figure 9.3). These remain subjective and debatable until clarified with segment-specific research on your customers' actual importance weightings and the behavioral impacts of each want or need. However, among the potentially most positive drivers of loyalty today is the tailored and personalized delivery of products, services, and touchpoint experiences.

You knew it was coming. No discussion of customer wants and needs would be complete without covering the growing customer demand for, "What I want, when I want, and how I want it!" Tailored or personalized delivery of products, services, and touch-point interactions are among the most powerful means to differentiate a firm today.

To actually deliver anything tailored and personalized, you must conduct extensive research with your customers to understand their specific loyalty-driving wants and the underlying needs. You must isolate those items that would be cost effective (because

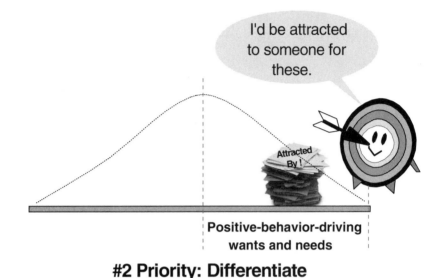

#2 Priority: Differentiate

Figure 9.3 Who stole my customers?? (positive levers).

tailored/personalized delivery is expensive) and then develop mass-customization capabilities to deliver them. Mass customization recognizes that what one person wants in a customized product or service is potentially wanted by many others, who make up a market segment. You can often develop such a delivery capability and get the economies of scale of mass production, while providing the appearance of tailored, personalized delivery. To do that requires extensive research for a pinpoint understanding of customers' requirements for personalization.

Having said that, their needs for personalization can be expected to fall into three major areas:

· **Targeted (not mass) marketing** can offer a highly effective means to interact with a customer, because these are pre-configured around value propositions known to be important and appeal to that specific consumer. As you have seen, even a telephone call at their home in the evening can be a positive event if relentlessly focused on real benefits to that customer.

· **Tailored, personalized products and services** (what/when/ how I want it) were once only a dream of wealthy, self-centric customers. Today this has become more of a reality and a common desire for many people. It began with the Internet and related new technical capabilities to provide electronic delivery of data to customers *their* way. This raised the customers' expectations from mere electronic delivery of individualized Web site screens, data, timing, and so on, to the personalized delivery of actual hard, manufactured products. This has extended to include a customer desire for channels beyond the Internet and for related customer-facing process experiences, "My way."

Note: The primary difference between tailored and personalized delivery versus needs-based segment delivery is in the level of delivery precision required (and therefore the costs). A walk-before-you-run sensibility dictates that most firms focus first on understanding their key, needs-based segments and then design products, services, and touchpoint experiences that will attract and keep those customers in key segments. Once this is done, it becomes possible to grow those capabilities to the greater level of precision and agility required to snap in a more personalized deliverable during a touchpoint interaction.

· **Treat me according to my unique value to you** is the third example of personalization. The "me" generation increasingly wants a balanced value proposition with their vendors, whereby the value to and from the customer are in synch. In this scenario, the desires of the customers are actually in line with those of the company. It is not economically illogical when customers say, "If I bought five cars here, I should not have to wait in line behind less loyal customers who contribute less to your profit."

The major problem today is that the value of a customer is often not known by a business, so they treat all customers the same and provide homogenous (same-cost) service to all (see Figure 9.4).

Figure 9.4 The value of a customer: Do you know which are high vs. low value?

Beyond the technical issues for a firm to determine the value of a customer (and enable appropriate treatment by employees with that data) there is often a great deal of pushback within management teams to the concept of different treatment to different groups of customers. Those situations provide great examples of how company culture and/or beliefs about your customers can impede your efforts to economically attract and retain customers. For example:

Culture. In a meeting with a major firm famous for customer service, I was told with great indignance that all their customers were equal and all received, and would always receive, the same great level of service. In the minds of those executives, identifying and treating high-value customers with an extraordinary service level was simply viewed as providing a poorer level of service to other customers. That would be contrary to their culture and strategy, which had enjoyed great success in the past. However, I believe that such a one-size-fits-all philosophy is fast becoming a going-out-of–business strategy. Why? Because either that one size is a high level that is unprofitable for your lower-value customer relationships, or it is set low and exposes you to lose your high-value customers. What worked yesterday, such as extraordinarily high service for everyone, is becoming untenable. Customer expectations are rising so fast that your limited resources can no longer keep up with their unlimited list of wants.

But, if you determine which customers are current or future high-value ones, you can afford to raise your cost of service for those, yet maintain a profitable relationship. For those high-profit customers, refer to the bell-shaped curve of behavior-driving needs and include both the left side, must-have, defection drivers and also the affordable right side, attractors and loyalty drivers.

For the lower value, less-profitable customers you must provide less-costly services, but ensure you meet their wants and needs expressed on the left side of the bell curve—their must-have, "*I'll leave if these aren't provided*" needs.

Treating customers according to their value to you can be done on an individual basis, such as private banking, or as a member of a high-value segment (gold, silver, platinum). But in all cases, you must provide a value to the customer that is cost-appropriate to the value you receive from that customer or segment.

Beliefs about their customers. Such beliefs, often formed without consulting the customers, also cause many organizations to resist a move to service levels based on the value of a customer. These businesses fail to seek out a path that could be mutually beneficial and acceptable to both the customer and the firm.

AIRLINES: HIGH-COST SERVICES FOR HIGH-VALUE CUSTOMERS

An executive of a one-size-fits-all corporation once leaped out of his chair and exclaimed to me, "Treat some of my customers differently? And it would be visible to others that these were treated better? My [automobile] customers would never stand for that!"

AIRLINES: HIGH-COST SERVICES FOR HIGH-VALUE CUSTOMERS (continued)

But, isn't that why airlines have designated different levels of frequent (loyal) flyers? Don't high-value, loyal airline customers receive higher-value service than others? What about those fancy lounges for their exclusive use? What about those special lines for express check-in? And the special toll-free telephone lines for gold, silver, and platinum customers to insure faster, customer-value-appropriate response?

Is that so wrong?

My response to that executive was to ask if he had ever noticed the shorter lines at airports for the high-value, frequent flyers? I asked if he had then walked down the concourse and heard music waft out the door of a carpeted lounge where more high-value frequent flyers were enjoying free drinks. Did he or his less fortunate fellow travelers march on the airline with flaming torches to demand equal treatment? No. Because they knew two things: the fortunate customers were the 4 percent who made up 80 percent of the airlines' profits, and he could obtain those same privileges by raising his own value. He could either become one of the 4 percent by increasing his business with the firm, or he could get the same services by paying for them—fly first class and/or buy a membership to their lounge.

For those who choose to do so, there are several fast-growing ways to personalize interactions, recognize the value of an individual, and insure a profitable relationship:

- Vary the levels of service and provide the high-cost, extraordinary, attractor wants and needs only to high-value customers, and provide lower-cost, basic, must-have needs to the low-value customers, or

- Vary the prices, and charge lower-value customers for high-cost services but make those free or lower-priced for high-value customers, or

- Vary both the levels and prices of services: offer several levels of service and prices and let the customer choose the level he or she wishes, but at a price that is commensurate with the value of that customer or segment.

Whichever approach a company implements, the treatment that a customer receives can be rationally linked to his or her value proposition to the business. High-value customers, in particular, expect to see that value reflected in your response to them. Customers are being conditioned to receive extraordinary benefits based on their personal value to the company (Hertz Gold, Marriott Platinum, United Airlines 1K, and so on) and they will bring that expectation, sooner or later, to the door of your business. Today that is a delighter that can attract customers (right side of the bell curve of needs and wants), but tomorrow it may well move to the left and become a must-have.

The likely question is: Will you give it to them now in order to attract customers . . . or later to keep the ones you have?

The Ultimate Need: A Solution—Not a Product, Not a Service

The preceding were a starter set of commonly cited customer needs that drive buying behavior. Your own research, with your own desired customer segments, can provide a more extensive list and additional design-level detail for the items in the starter set. However, one more concept must be discussed as you move forward to find product and/or service designs to address your customers' wants and needs: *solutions*.

A natural tendency is for a firm to think in terms of a product response to customer needs, or a service(s) response. That is a trap. It limits your thinking and it takes your focus away from the underlying customer value system to which you wish to appeal. Because at the end of the day, what the customer wants is neither a product nor a service: The customer wants resolution to his or her problem, issue, or desire. And in that context, your offering is more properly thought of as a solution, not a product or service. By doing so, you keep your design requirements and your customers' needs at the forefront of your thinking.

There has been an evolution of thought regarding the value proposition between vendors and customers—initially it was product features and benefits. Then, in the 1980s, the quality movement provided a means to further differentiate one's products based upon a perceived quality factor, so producers often wrapped their product offerings in a quality-focused marketing message.

Toward the end of the '90s, quality became less of an issue, products became more similar and easy to copy, and business strategy had shifted to service(s) as a new basis for differentiation. The target, however, remained focused on the product (see Figure 9.5).

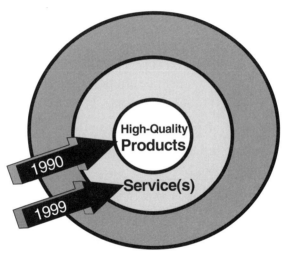

Figure 9.5 Differentiation in the 1990s: Enhance products with service(s).

As airline seats, hotel rooms, and mutual funds looked pretty much the same, service became the means to add value, attract/ retain customers, and build market share. With the Internet came the capabilities to make that service delivery more and more personalized. With additional technologies, such as massive terabyte databases coupled with data mining for pinpoint accuracy, concepts such as micro-marketing and mass-customization of products and services became increasingly practical. The value of the service ring depicted in Figure 9.5 increased with each break-through in service delivery. An airplane seat, a hotel room, mutual funds, brokerage transactions, all could be upgraded in terms of customer value by leveraging the service ring. Tailored, personalized, customized delivery of what the customer wants at touchpoints became a major lever to drive customer loyalty by the year 2000.

What's next?

The answer is: a fundamental shift of target away from products to a focus on *solutions* to the customer's underlying problems, issues, or desires (see Figure 9.6). Business strategy must change to emphasize and *solve the customer's issue or need,* rather than continue to try to fit a product to a customer or to surround a product with attractive service.

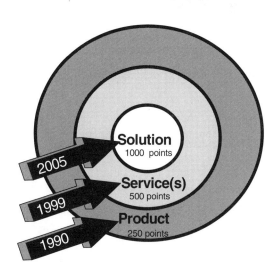

Figure 9.6 The value proposition of the 2000s: Product + service = solution.

A valuable lesson was taught to me early in my consulting career: Vendors with a product resemble someone with a hammer who then approaches their customer by looking for a problem that resembles a nail.

If you have a product (i.e., the hammer), you tend to see your customers' issues through that lens and start to look for "nails" to provide a use for your hammer. But if you approach your customers from a viewpoint that seeks to identify and provide solutions to their needs, you potentially offer a far greater value proposition to them (Figure 9.6).

We end the discussion of envisioning ideal delivery of loyalty-driving needs with this recap: Find out not only what they want (a product or service articulated) but why (the underlying value or benefit they can receive). Focus on the "why" they want it, and as you design, deliver, and market your offering, customer-facing process, or channel, keep it defined as a solution—not a product, not a service. By doing so, you are most likely to deliver the ultimate possible value to your customer.

You Are the Customer

What about when you are the customer?

Can you envision things that would determine your loyalty other than price?

What are your must-have needs? How important is courtesy to you? Can you remember the last time you were really impressed by the attitudes of employees of a firm? Did it make you return? Are there companies whose images in your mind are actually the attitudes of their employees? (Have you ever flown with Jet Blue or Southwest Airlines?)

What about when you are highly irritated by the negative attitude of employees or management of a firm? Have you ever said you would never do business there again due to such an experience? How might they have handled that situation in a manner that would have retained you?

What about competency? When do you feel you are dealing with competent contact points? What makes you most comfortable with someone with whom you are dealing? What would cause you to no longer do business there due to employees' competency? How could a firm attract and retain you because of the attributes and competency of their people, rather than their products?

What about a knowledgeable contact? How much information regarding the firm's products or services do you expect? When I test drove and then took delivery of my Chrysler Town and Country, I had to show the salesperson how to operate several features of the vehicle. In such a transactional relationship, I did not expect him to have knowledge of me, but I did expect minimum knowledge of the product and of their sales and delivery processes.

What are your expectations? Do they differ based on the type of product or type of relationship involved? Are some situations transactional relationships in your mind and not an ongoing relationship where they should have knowledge of you?

Could even transactional relationships be of greater value to you if they had more information about you?

What about responsiveness? Can you remember the last time you were so impressed with a firm's timing or turnaround that it caused you to return? Why? How did it reflect an understanding of your needs or urgency as a customer? Can you recall a time when someone demonstrated their flexibility to work with you? Can you remember, instead, someone citing inflexible practices or "That's not our policy"?

Do any of these impact your loyalty and willingness to return? To defect?

Do you expect the treatment or services you receive to be reflective of the amount of business that you bring to that relationship? Your high-volume purchases often receive a reduced price that reflects the size and value of the transaction or relationship. Do you think your value should also be evident during touchpoints experienced when you acquire, pay for, and receive post-sell service for those products?

What if you are an intermittent or low-dollar customer, would it bother you to know that other customers with higher volumes get preferred or expedited treatment? If so, would it help if these were also available to you, but at a price that was related to your overall business with the firm?

Do you see firms today that try to gain your loyalty and repeat business? How?

Are your expectations of companies growing in this regard?

Which is most likely to attract you when you are looking for something to fill a need: (1) A product, (2) A service, or (3) A solution, or a combination of products and services, configured around your need?

- What about *your* customers? What are they seeing you do in this regard?
- What are your competitors doing to **steal away** your customers? What should *you* be doing?

10

What You Must Do: Institutionalize Loyalty

G ood intentions, and even good management, are not good enough. Make that your mantra and a design point for your business improvements.

First, your firm needs methodical approaches to secure actionable customer wants and needs. These must be systematic, ongoing business processes that identify and target desired market segments, then capture and monitor ongoing changes in the loyalty-driving wants and needs for those segments.

Second, your firm must also have a management system with standardized processes that relentlessly use the customers' needs—and feedback on performance—to drive the design, operation, and metrics of success for the business. This includes the company infrastructure (processes, organization, and technology) as well as the culture, cross functional and enterprise wide. Without such measures to orchestrate changes based on your customers' input, there can be no significant results, only good intentions.

TRANSFORMING A BUSINESS: *CLICK HERE* TO CHANGE CULTURES

I met on a Friday afternoon with the president of a major firm in Taiwan who wanted to transform his business from a focus on the commercial, corporate marketplace to an orientation around consumers. Ironically, representatives of a popular software brand that claimed to do just that had been in to see him that morning and were scheduled to meet the following day with his CEO.

The president said that he expected to sign a contract with the software company, but as a courtesy he had not canceled our appointment. So we used the time to discuss the experiences of some firms that had attempted similar, dramatic transformations— particularly IBM's experience.

He asked several questions about IBM's hardware and software capabilities to support a customer initiative or focus. I attempted to answer him, but emphasized the importance of also changing the

TRANSFORMING A BUSINESS: *CLICK HERE* TO CHANGE CULTURES (continued)

business processes, organization, and culture to align with that technology. As our discussion progressed, the president became somewhat animated, then visibly agitated and finally outright concerned. The issues and experiences I had shared caused him to doubt the wisdom of the session the next day with his CEO and the software firm.

"The software people told me they have a packaged application that will transform us into a customer-focused firm and enable us to penetrate the consumer market!" he exclaimed. "But, you say that our processes and other infrastructure must also be changed, and that culture is our greatest risk. The software firm did not say any of this!"

The president then quickly revised the Saturday schedule and arranged for two, successive (dueling) presentations to be made to his CEO:

1. A software firm that claimed their technology could transform a major organization

2. A global hardware, software, and services firm that cautioned that no one's (not even their own) technology can transform an organization without changes to align and link the related business processes, organization, metrics of success, and culture.

As we left the president's office, my colleague from Taipei whispered to me, "No wonder such a high percentage of customer strategies fail."

Implementation of a customer initiative requires more than statements of your new direction, policies, or practices and a magical software application. Most will need major investments in business infrastructure and, whether lengthy, complex, costly, or not, will also require changes in management and employee behavior. These collectively make your customer-focused initiatives into institutionalized walk-the-walk reality, rather than mere talk-the-talk platitudes. Firms with actual experience found these much easier to say than do and can provide you with valuable lessons learned.

As an example, most books on customer relationship topics dwell on the technologies available today and the challenges to integrate those new designs with a firm's legacy systems, processes, and organization. A critical, overriding issue, however, is how these all come together, not via design, but their social and cultural implementation, i.e., change management. Such critical knowledge can best be gained through experience, including what other firms have learned *not* to do, as well as what they have found worked well.

IBM was involved in such a ten-year learning experience, as it transformed from one of the world's premier product houses to a more customer-focused, services and solutions firm. To be candid, much of what was learned occurred during a painful period in the 1990s when little progress was made. During that time of limited successes, and often actual failures, IBM gained valuable insights on what not to do. In later years, as IBM began to reap the benefits of the transformation, executives of other firms often asked to hear about the disappointments on the journey before hearing what worked well. Those senior managers knew the value of learning from the mistakes, as well as the successes, of others.

The following are critical findings (both positive and negative) during the transformation of IBM, which was ultimately incredibly successful (see Figure 10.1). These are a matter of personal opinion and, as with the rest of this book, are respectfully offered as such.

Lessons Learned

▸ I. A Case for Action and Buy-In
        vs. LACK OF URGENCY !!!

▸ II. Actionable Customer Input
        vs. WE KNOW WHAT CUSTOMERS WANT !!!

▸ III. Enterprise-Wide Executive Ownership
        vs. OPTIMIZE MY SILO !!!

▸ IV. Cultural Transformation and Teaming
        vs. KNOWLEDGE IS POWER !!!

Figure   10.1   What has experience taught?

Lesson 1: A Case for Action and Buy-In (vs. Lack of Urgency!)

A key finding during IBM's transformation, and supported by experiences with global clients, is that business change cannot be legislated. While it is possible to design new processes, organization, and technology, these are meaningless unless embraced by employees and management. If your employees' behaviors do not change regarding the use of these new infrastructure items, then nothing changes from the perspective of your customers.

The experiences at IBM can provide you with valuable insights on "where not to step" as well as where to find more firm ground to begin your journey.

For example, if your company has a history of repeated changes of management, all-too-regular reorganization announcements, or the use of annual themes to rally employees and kick off the new year, then your exciting new strategic direction may be perceived as merely another program de jour. A "this, too, shall pass" mindset may permeate your mid- and lower-echelon employees who will then hide and wait for this one, also, to pass. This was certainly true at IBM, where all of the above were common, plus a history existed that said *vision* or *strategy* is fluffy-stuff and never actually implemented.

Extraordinary product successes (as noted in Chapter 1) had bred complacency and arrogance: Why change? Aren't we already the best?

IBM's employee-focused culture had also created a job-for-life environment: Employees literally could remove a manager quite easily, but the manager faced a daunting road to secure removal of an employee. In that era, HR at IBM was definitely human relations, not human resources, and the personnel department was quick to take the side of the employee. The upside and purpose of that carefully crafted culture was that employees had little interest in, or need for, a union. The downside was that there was little motivation for an employee to do anything he or she resisted, and if two or more shared that view, their power was significantly more than their manager's.

Into this environment (*programs de jour; power to the employee; this, too, shall pass*) IBM tried to introduce new processes and technologies in the early 1990s with little measurable results. If your firm plans to embark on such a journey with new customer-focused strategies, you must consider the similarities in your own environment and how to get management and employee buy-in to the need for such changes.

For IBM, the solution was to establish a *Case for Action* (the business justification to move from the status quo) that would clearly communicate both the new direction as well as a compelling need for change. Management learned that the two components should be carefully crafted and tightly linked:

1. **Communicate the customer strategy linked to business strategy.**

Employees must understand the difference between the new initiative and other, less critical things they have heard from management. To do this, the CEO or senior-most executive must personally establish the effort within a context of the business strategy and clearly communicate it as a key enabler and critical element of that strategy.

2. Communicate a catalyst for the change: why this trip is necessary.

Changes of such magnitude are typically either vision-driven (a great new idea) or crisis-driven (a matter of survival). Employees must understand and agree with such a need, in order to be willing to proactively help implement it. Without such buy-in, resistance can take many forms, with passive resistance being the most difficult to recognize, much less address. Negative rewards and punishments, for example, are hard to administer to passive resistors, who can easily undermine the effort of a new program in protective transparency.

Perhaps more problematic than the employees are mid-level managers, who often are the greatest source of passive resistance because they may feel the most threatened. For example, a truly customer-focused initiative will often empower customer-facing employees and flatten the organization chart to speed decision-making at the front line. Whose jobs are threatened when an organizational pyramid is to be flattened? Middle managers. So, what is the actual message that reaches the lower levels of your firm, after it passes through this middle tier? If the message comes from, and is daily reinforced by, the CEO then even the passive resistors will have minimal impact.

A powerful way to communicate a crisis-driven initiative is to provide anecdotal evidence of the crisis and the need for change. The IBM example demonstrates how dramatic changes in employee behavior and buy-in can be accomplished. Part and parcel with execution of the transformation was the repeated communication of IBM's negative customer feedback (for example, video-taped sessions between the IBM CEO and customers) and the precipitous drop in market capitalization, stock price, and shareholder value. At one point, the value of the great IBM company had dropped to the point that the firm was exposed to the possibility of an acquisition or takeover. Customers were leaving. Employees' jobs were in jeopardy because the company was in danger. These are things an employee can understand, but only if they are candidly communicated.

In such an environment, in fact, not only was active resistance no longer politically correct, but even passive resistance became more visible and less tolerated by peer employees (or peer managers), who began to support, and even want, removal of deadwood from the organization.

Lesson 2: Actionable Customer Input (vs. We Know What Customers Want!)

This lesson learned might also be called *When Good People Have Bad Ideas.*

A common phrase heard inside and outside of IBM has been, "We know what our customers want and need!" With this as their foundation, good people often embark on poorly grounded initiatives. Good people. Bad idea.

The more time and money a firm has spent to understand its customers, the more it thinks it "knows." The problem is that a firm can unknowingly conduct its customer-view data collection while using an inside-out focus that biases the data.

For example, a company's management traditionally develops the questions on the firm's customer surveys. Good managers with good intentions will insist that such surveys contain questions regarding their own particular products, services, or functional areas. But, these may not include the touchpoints or experiences that actually impact a customer's future buying behavior. Such questions serve to waste an opportunity for precious feedback, and negative customer satisfaction responses on these can distract management's focus and misdirect scarce resources away from true loyalty drivers.

Even when these managers learn that customers have dramatically new or different wants or needs, companies can be biased against changing an existing satisfaction survey to reflect the new items. When research found that satisfaction surveys at IBM contained items that no longer related to customer loyalty, and failed to include some key items that did, the immediate reaction by several managers was to resist change. "What," they exclaimed, "and lose a 20-year trend-line on all those old questions?" Their own research methods and biases had more momentum, power, and influence than the actual voice of the customer. Ultimately, the voice of reason from more senior executives won the day, and IBM invested to obtain more actionable customer feedback on survey questions that were important to customers and their loyalty.

To begin to obtain such customer feedback, IBM first identified the touchpoint interactions that potentially have the highest value to customers, and thereby the greatest leverage to control their decisions to return. Company thinking regarding touchpoints changed from moments of truth, to moments of value, and to have those key moments identified by customers, not employees.

Next, was recognition that the marketplace is comprised of many groupings of people, or segments, and each of these can have very different needs or value propositions than other segments at those moments. IBM had previously segmented their customers based on the products or channels they used (and industry, for commercial customers), rather than on the underlying needs and wants that drive those decisions. Segmenting customers based on such criteria merely provided a surrogate for their needs—it described their buying behavior rather than understanding why. IBM found that knowledge of the underlying wants and needs common within each segment offered the company an opportunity to deliver in a manner that generates loyalty.

There are many marketing research approaches that will statistically reduce the risks and ensure the profitable benefits of customer segmentation. However, there is often a need to take immediate action, interim to more rigorous and time-consuming research. In IBM's case, as market share and stock prices plummeted, there was a critical need to identify some target groups of customers and take immediate action before investing in extensive research. In this walk-before-you-run example, IBM used a simple method to start the work, one that you might also find useful for your business.

To get focused quickly, IBM management brainstormed ideas on how to divide their marketplace into groups most likely to have needs-based segmentation when engaged in a buying transaction. In your own business, for example, what are the dramatically different ways that your customers either make their buying decisions or approach their buying investment/expense? IBM management agreed there were (at least) three different types of buying behavior that denoted very different underlying value systems, wants, and needs. The three types of buying behavior and examples of underlying customer needs that your customers may also share include:

1. **Off the rack**—Some customers want the convenience, lower cost, and lack of risk associated with purchasing standardized, tried-and-true products. Depending on the product or service being acquired, off-the-rack purchasers can often have very different motivations that drive their purchase decisions and—potentially—their loyalty. If the product is high tech, for example, their value system is often oriented around risk avoidance as they let others be the innovators who take the lead. Off-the-rack purchasers are, at best, fast followers. By grouping your customers who demonstrate this type of behavior, your firm can begin a process to obtain their outside-in vision of an ideal, off-the-rack vendor. You can then optimize *their* value proposition, or why they buy off the rack, for *your* business.

2. **Tailored**—Some customers want the benefits of having a standardized product, or basic platform, but modified to better fit their own characteristics. These concepts can apply to simple retail goods, such as a pair of pants, as well as complex technological products and services, such as information technology or manufacturing equipment. Buying uncuffed slacks or a generic CRM application and then tuning it to their needs can provide value propositions such as short lead-times, low cost, and reduced risk, when compared to a custom-made, individually crafted alternative. Once you understand their underlying need for flexibility behind such buying behavior, you can optimize your delivery for the customers in this needs-based segment.

3. **Custom crafted**—Then there are the customers who want a one-of-a-kind, personally crafted item to meet their unique wants and needs. Perhaps they are innovators, who have shunned a fast-follower strategy in their business (or consumer lifestyle) and intend to be the trendsetter. Perhaps their wants, needs, and application of the product are truly unique. Whatever the motivation, it is critical that you understand and appeal to it for each individual customer in this segment.

By dividing your customers into the groups that relate to your own business (not IBM's), you can probe for each group's vision of you as their ideal provider. A critical point for you here is that most of your beliefs about customers, including what you learn from visioning exercises with such segments, are merely hypotheses.

IBM and other companies used such subjective data when circumstances and timeframes demanded immediate action, but in the long run more objective and statistically valid research was ultimately obtained with the assistance of qualified marketing research experts.

An array of research techniques were used that can also benefit you. For example, most firms attempt to determine the importance of the individual customer's needs by asking the customer, "How important is this?" and presenting a scale such as 1–10. A more precise measure of business impact of each customer need or want can be statistically derived by correlating customers' satisfaction levels for each item versus their actual behaviors. For example, did a group of customers unhappy with a particular need/want stay or leave? An important point for you is that the end result is your ability to have questions on your satisfaction surveys that your customers feel are important to their buying decision. The bell-shaped curve (see Figure 9.1 on page 122) of customer behavior-driving needs and wants can then be constructed and used for your decision-making and investments.

IBM found that efforts to link those needs back to and improve the infrastructure creates immense data. A valuable lesson learned is that to be truly actionable, the firm must have methodical ways to identify, organize, and then manage such customer needs and wants linkages all the way through to the implementation of the enabling infrastructure.

Quality Function Deployment (QFD) is a Japanese-originated management tool or method to identify, track, and control such complexity and design a product based on customer input. IBM found those approaches useful, but hard to manually orchestrate, and the automated tools for QFD on the market were intended for development of products, not processes or company infrastructure. At IBM, Cindy Adiano developed and patented an innovative QFD-based analytical tool that became a valuable enabler for internal customer-focused initiatives and external client consulting. Depending on the size and complexity of your processes and customer data, a manual or automated QFD-like approach can also provide your firm with a powerful improvement vehicle.

Lesson 3: Enterprise-Wide Executive Ownership (vs. Optimize My Silo!)

Among the most difficult transformation issues encountered by IBM were sponsorship and governance. It may seem obvious that sponsorship should be from the very top and that governance ("How things are done around here") should appear in published roles or responsibilities and be documented in standardized, ongoing processes. However, this has been a consistent issue in most firms that attempt a major transformation.

As far back as the Quality movement of the '80s and '90s, it was common to hear management gurus speak of "lighting a thousand little fires" from within the middle of the organization, which were expected to spread enterprise-wide. They encouraged the development of respected, mid-level employees and managers as champions and pioneers who would promote the movement from within by using influence rather than actual authority. This sounded good to senior managers, who had other things with which to deal and did not wish to be involved. Besides, they reasoned, the truly great ideas would bubble to the top.

The approach was doomed to failure—at least within IBM and many other major corporations. Those pioneer-influencers were stranded, powerless in a hostile environment, and often only the very gifted and/or fortunate survived.

Why? Because almost any business outcome (or customer experience) is the culmination of several tasks or activities (a process) and involves more than one person. Several people who often reside in different functions or organizations usually perform such processes. Institutionalized knowledge is required, because it is not simply "in one person's head" how to accomplish the customer-desired result. Immediately, several conflicting forces come into play:

· Resistance to the standardization and documentation of activities required for processes to be consistently performed by multiple parties and organizations.

· Resistance to behavioral changes required to implement standardized processes.

· Resistance to subsume the interests of one organization (or function) in order to optimize the multi-organizational, cross-functional value chain or process.

Here is where even the great ideas die and do not rise to the top, because individuals, organizations, or functions are often threatened by such ideas. Virtually every great idea for an enterprise has some potential negative effect or impact on the self-interest of a smaller element of the firm. The managers and workforces of most companies are organized and motivated to optimize smaller, specialized units or elements, all the way down to an individual employee or producer. When the *great idea* is to eliminate or radically modify an organization, function, manager, or employee to make the overall enterprise more efficient, effective, or customer-preferred, then the threatened subset often stops the progress.

This can occur any place between a customer-facing or desk-level employee up to, and including, the senior-most business unit executive.

Not only did small-scale quality initiatives often sputter during the '80s and '90s at IBM and other companies, but the more fundamental reengineering in the mid-to-late '90s also was often mismanaged and failed. Ironically, it was the *management structure* adopted by IBM and other firms to facilitate a successful change that was often the toxic element that doomed them. Most firms saw an initiative to transform their capabilities and culture as being far afield of their own business competencies, so they established such ventures as project offices. The idea was to centralize a staff, or center of competency, with the specialized skills required to reengineer business processes and effect the technological or organizational changes that would be required. Often a respected manager was selected from within the firm to head the center as a change agent, and to demonstrate the company's commitment the best and brightest were taken from each function as a core team.

So far so good. New skills and organization were required to implement the new strategy or initiative, and the company responded. Next, such firms typically reported their project office to a staff executive, and that was where such ventures started to fall apart.

EXECUTIVE OWNERSHIP: LINE VS. STAFF

The leader of a reengineering center of competency at a major corporation in the Pacific Rim had this problem. The gentleman was a year or two away from retirement and, before his appointment to a staff role, had distinguished himself as a business unit executive. The firm was one of the largest organizations in that country (second only to the army), and its market had been opened up by legislation to new competitors. They were experts in the technologies of their particular industry, not in attracting and retaining customers. Almost immediately they began to lose customers.

The new competency project leader had been given liberal funding to construct a methodology to engineer the company to be more attractive to customers. He personally reported to the CEO in order to send a signal all the way down to the desk-level employee that this initiative was important and not just the program du jour. He had

EXECUTIVE OWNERSHIP: LINE VS. STAFF (continued)

been provided a staff comprised of the best people in their corporation, who were taken out of their business units, and he had supplemented that by hiring outside expert academics and business practitioners of process reengineering.

Still, after a period of almost two years, there was little or no measurable progress and, in fact, customer perception and loyalty were worse than ever. Within the firm much had been designed to improve customer loyalty, but little had been successfully implemented. The new processes they envisioned crossed multiple functions and organizations. The people who performed tasks within any one process resided in several different organizational units, or silos, each headed by a different senior executive. And those executives were not only autonomous from one another, they fought among themselves for scarce corporate resources, personal recognition, and/or to optimize their business unit— even if it meant negatively impacting other units.

The most visible sponsor or leader of the initiatives was a staff person, trying to secure cross-organizational change. Given the absence of any cross-functional management structure (governance), there was little likelihood that employees would change their behaviors and begin dramatic new levels of cross-silo cooperation to make the new processes and procedures work.

The firm ultimately looked for others, with experience in such matters, for knowledge on how to proceed.

Early in its effort to reengineer, IBM also experienced sponsorship and governance issues that provide a painful "this didn't work well for us" lesson to share. A highly respected, senior-line executive had been appointed to a staff position that reported to the IBM CEO. The senior executive managed a center of competency, comprised of top thinkers from across the company, empowered to develop and lead the implementation of major process changes. However, after two years there was little actual progress, but a lot of finger-pointing. No one, it seemed, was willing to make the sacrifices required for actual implementation of what was perceived as *someone else's* program. And top-line executives seemed unable to get it resolved, because it required cooperation between senior folks with little history (or incentive) to play well with others and share their toys.

What was the solution at IBM? Ownership of and responsibility to improve key business processes (which flow across multiple line organizations) were assigned to those very line executives. Each key line executive was made responsible for a single process to own and improve, even though that process crossed, and was performed within, the other line executives' functional areas.

As a result, the senior executive responsible for the sales process also had to cooperate and work with the other senior managers, who now owned sister processes, because those other executives' employees also performed critical portions of the sales process, and vice versa.

Still, a major source of continued friction and contention was IBM's fragmented and far-flung information technology (IT) resource. Virtually every major change envisioned for a process had an absolute dependency on data to be provided within the new process what/where/when needed. Debates on the best use of limited IT resources literally stopped all progress, as the IBM culture (at that time) allowed almost any key executive the ability to non-concur, while few could cast the decisive positive vote.

Ultimately, after a change in CEOs, a fundamental change was made to break the logjam: the role of a Super Chief Information Officer (CIO) was established. This corporate officer would not only control the key transformational enabler, IT, but also had the overriding responsibility to drive and coordinate IBM's business transformation, enterprise-wide. This took the most critical source of contention (scarce IT resource) out of the hands of individual organizations or processes and insured that the transformation would not be suboptimized by silo thinking.

Ultimately, a governance (or management) system for an optimized business, enterprise-wide, and key business processes were defined, standardized, and documented. Once that structure became institutionalized from top to bottom, real change resulted and the ghosts and memory of the early, mid-level pioneers faded away.

Lesson 4: Cultural Transformation and Teaming (vs. Knowledge Is Power!)

Beyond infrastructure (governance, processes, organization, and technology), the most critical element in successful transformation is culture. Culture within a firm affects both how it perceives the world (company view vs. customer view) as well as how it reacts and behaves. This includes how employees sense and respond not only to customers but also to other employees. Some of the many cultural issues and biases IBM faced, which may prove valuable lessons learned for you, included a need to move:

- From an internal point of view (inside-out) to an external (outside-in) viewpoint and recognize the customer as the ultimate expert, no matter how great the level of internal skill and experience within the IBM company.

- From a product and services mentality to a solutions mindset (how your customers see products and services), including the service element or component of every touchpoint interaction.

- From a silo focus (vertical organization chart and performance) to a process view (horizontal process flow, multi-organizational), because things customers want or need tend to be the result of cumulative, cross-functional activities.

- From individual employee performance to team-based successes, because critical processes that deliver customer needs are implemented by several people who collectively determine success.

- From an individual executive's business unit performance to business-wide metrics, because processes are made up of

people from potentially different vertical line units, and
executives collectively impact cross-organizational
enterprise-wide results.

· From knowledge as power (rewarding the expert for
hoarding) to knowledge as assets (rewarding the team-player
for sharing).

A key element to accomplish the above was teaming. Process performance required a team effort, but IBM had traditionally
valued, emphasized, and rewarded individual accomplishment.
An entirely new value system was put into place that emphasized
teaming and cooperation, both at the top and at the desk levels,
by linking personal compensation to the collective performance
of the new processes the people jointly impacted. In fact, at that
point the fortunes of the IBM company began to turn as
employee and executive incentives were shifted from individual
employee or organization performance to more collective results,
such as overall business growth and customer results.

After Lou Gerstner became the CEO, there was clear, senior-most
executive sponsorship, not a reliance on mid-tier pioneers. The
executives whose employees made up the bulk of the processes
now owned them, via a governance structure with incentives for
both the executives and employees to team and cooperate. Those
executives, unlike the earlier influence-peddling pioneers, had
both the responsibility and authority to affect the necessary
changes. An 80/20 philosophy for compensation (80 percent
based on your unit's performance, 20 percent on other) was

effectively reversed, as enterprise-wide and customer metrics took a larger role.

Perhaps the most effective thing done to change the culture was to obtain actionable, customer-defined input on things truly important to customers, and tie that relentlessly to everyone's compensation. Until the last half of the 1990s, IBM had never officially had a "lay off" of employees. However, with the new, crisis-driven case for action laid out by Gerstner, the final lever was pulled to obtain changed behavior and a new IBM culture: Employees were rated, then ranked, and the bottom10 percent of many organizations were terminated. And the criteria for determining ratings and rankings were structured to be inexorably customer focused and team based.

Customer-related metrics became the primary indicators of success and the basis for financial incentives. The word *customer* became the single most often used in the company. Not only was compensation tied to it, but also survival as a company and as an employee.

At that point, teaming became a critical element; without it, the individual employee could not reap customer-metric-based rewards. Employees had to establish measurable, customer-focused, personal business objectives, and their performance on those criteria was appraised primarily by their peers, not their managers. Teaming and team-based skills quickly became a matter of individual survival, and later a means for personal (based on team performance) success. This was an incredible shift for a company that had been founded on a sales culture that valued and rewarded individual performance. The old job-for-life culture was ended. The new, customer-focused, team-based culture was kick-started.

In such a culture, knowledge was valued as an enterprise asset and shared across the company. This behavior was encouraged, incentivized, and enabled via supporting processes and infrastructure. At IBM, a huge investment was made to facilitate knowledge creation and a knowledge-sharing environment. This was done both organizationally and technologically.

Organizationally, functions were created with specialized skills to promote the creation, capturing, and sharing of knowledge assets. Chief Knowledge Officer (CKO), for example, is a formal position to ensure that leading-edge approaches, processes, and technology are in place. But it is via more informal, loosely organized structures that the actual work gets done and the results are realized. Sharenets of professional employees with a common area of expertise or passion have been formed. An example might be a sharenet around a particular high-value competency or capability such as IT strategy or customer loyalty management. While each of these sharenets has a formally designated leader, there is no further direct-line relationship between the leader and the members. Members do not report or answer to the sharenet leader. In fact, the leader is more of an enabler for them, rather than vice versa, and is responsible to see that their collective knowledge continues to be grown, documented, shared, and exploited to the fullest, company-wide.

In IBM, a sharenet leader often establishes a core team, or inner circle, comprised of several of the more expert or passionate practitioners, willing to devote time and energy because it increases their skills as well as value to the company—and to their clients. A more extensive set of global practitioners is identified who will also use that knowledge, and the entire loosely structured entity is tied together with a *technological* enabler: the intellectual capital management system. The sharenet core group determines what is intellectual capital and what is not. They are gatekeepers who insure the quality and relevance of the data. The data itself is accessible via Lotus Notes, worldwide, as well as the ability for any member of the sharenet to communicate with any or all others.

Examples of how company knowledge is furthered include primary and secondary research projects by the leader on topics that increase the skills of sharenet members. Additionally, innovative new approaches and techniques used in external client services engagements and internal business initiatives are harvested and documented by the members for reuse by others in the sharenet.

A consultant in Switzerland can access the most recent valuable experiences of colleagues in Asia Pacific or the U.S., for example, during a complex client engagement. She or he can also have instant electronic communication with the person who originally placed the intellectual capital onto the sharenets databases. Plus, sharenet members can be given the capability to make real-time changes or updates to old data.

The extent to which employees contribute to such shared knowledge (and not be mere library card holders who use the data) has a major impact on their peer review appraisals, ratings, and rankings. At IBM, such teaming and knowledge sharing are now integral to, and a key part of the fabric of, a customer-centric and customer-preferred firm.

Summary: Learning from Experience

When market share and stock prices plummeted, IBM was forced to ask, "**Who stole my customer??**"

Although other businesses had attracted away market share, IBM ultimately learned that the actual culprit behind lost customers is often "*us*"—a firm's own culture, past successes, and prior strengths.

Today, as your business looks for the causes behind your customer attrition, the likely answer is, at least in part, *the enemy is you*. Even if you have the best of intentions, customers are unintentionally driven away by your lack of awareness and orientation around their rapidly changing needs. In this environment your customer can easily leave or be attracted (**stolen**) away by a firm that flexibly aligns its culture, touchpoints, and products around your customers' dynamic needs and wants.

The concepts and experience-based lessons that have been shared in this book can help you to *keep your customers in this era of* (increasingly) *easy defection*.

You Are the Customer

What about when you are the customer?

Can you think of times when you were clearly dealing with a firm that had not yet learned some of the key lessons in this chapter to institutionalize being customer focused?

Lesson 1: A Case for Action and Buy-In (vs. Lack of Urgency)

For example, regarding employee buy-in: Have you ever gone into a business after your expectations were set by their advertising, and then had a very different experience? Did their people not seem to be in synch with their brand image or message? Were you ready to be delighted, but it didn't happen?

When that happens, does it reflect on the individual or the firm? Do you tend to think, "My, what a poor employee," or do you more naturally think that's just bad management?

What about the importance of enterprise-wide employee performance? Have you ever had a positive experience with the sales personnel of a firm, and then had a quite different experience later with their service department? Or dealt with the same people, but received different treatment during their post-sell interactions? What did you think about that company?

How would a more consistent, enterprise-wide, customer focus and sense of urgency have impacted your perception of that business?

When are you most likely to return to buy again from a firm? Is it when a particular department delights you, although another area falls short, or is it more likely to be when you sense a cross-organizational consistency in treatment?

So, how important is employee buy-in to a firm's customer-focused culture and programs when *you* are the customer?

- Now, what about *your* customers?
- Have your employees bought-in to your efforts 100 percent to be customer focused?
- What are you doing to insure that your employees are providing your customers with a consistent, high-quality, customer-focused experience, enterprise-wide?
- How do you establish in the minds of your employees a uniform vision of the importance of the customer, of your customer strategies and initiatives, and of their roles to fulfill those strategies?
- How would your customers answer these questions about your firm?

Lesson 2: Actionable Customer Input (vs. We Know What Customers Want!)

What about a firm's knowledge of your needs and wants when you are the customer? Have you dealt with someone who did not appear to be listening? Can you think of situations where they seemed to be waiting for you to stop talking (or they simply just interrupt) so they can tell you what you want? How does that make you feel?

Would you go back to a doctor who consistently came into the examination room and began to tell you how you feel and what you need? How about a financial advisor who did that? How about a consultant who did that?

Now, how would you feel about a firm that, as they began a relationship with you, made it a point to learn what was important to you? What if they asked why you want their products or services, or your desired attributes of their touchpoint interactions and then designed those to meet not only your wants but also your underlying needs? What if knowledge of your needs was reflected in all interactions with their employees and channels of access? When you are the customer, how valuable would it be to have such experiences that way—your way?

Could such a vendor **steal** away your business?

- How are you doing that with your firm and for *your* customers?

- Do you rely on past knowledge and your historic point of view as to what customers want and need? Or do you methodically acquire actionable, current knowledge of the individual customer as well as market segments?
- How do your touchpoints reflect this?
- How do employees use this?
- How do customers experience it?

Lesson 3: Enterprise-Wide Executive Ownership (vs. Optimize My Silo!)

When you are the customer, what are your expectations when dealing with the different silos, departments, organizations, or lines of business in a company? Have there been times you felt that one part of a company considered itself a separate firm, rather than part of a team? Have you:

- Ever spent a considerable sum with one portion of a company, only to be treated as a stranger elsewhere in the firm?
- Ever felt that one part of a business was trying to optimize or exploit your profitability without regard to your full, enterprise-wide value?
- Had to fill out another complete set of customer applications, with your mother's maiden name, and so on, when you have already done so elsewhere in their company; for example, at a home loan department of a bank where you already have accounts with their deposits, investments, or credit card units?

Did you ever notice that "things are done differently around here," depending on the organization with which you are dealing within a company? Did you ever call one customer contact center only to be told to redial to another center that's attached to another function in their firm? For example, my wife called our local inn to make dinner reservations, only to be told she had reached their lodge room reservations and to hang up and redial a different number for the restaurant. Has something similar happened to you?

How many times an evening must that occur to a potential customer? What must they be thinking to not establish a capability to transfer such calls? ("Why can't those darned customers get it right? I have to tell them to hang up and redial a dozen times a night. What stupid customers.")

When you are the customer, how important is it to deal with a single enterprise and not be bounced between autonomous organizations?

- What about *your* customers?
- What do they experience with your business? Is it one firm?
- Do you allow (maybe even reward) your silos to optimize themselves, possibly to the detriment of the overall organization?
- How do you promote an emphasis to consistently optimize the overall business, rather than a portion of the business? How do you insure that the interests of a person,

department, or function will be relentlessly subsumed to the interest of the larger firm?

- Do you manage your business horizontally, so that the outputs of one part of the firm (say, the sales department) are also ideal inputs to the next part of your business (say, manufacturing, billing, or delivery)? Are all departments aligned and linked to provide what customers want?

- What would your customers say about you?

Lesson 4: Cultural Transformation and Teaming (vs. Knowledge Is Power!)

When you are a customer, can you sense when you are dealing with employees of a business as individuals versus when they are culturally aligned and linked as a team? How is that apparent to you? When do you most notice it? Is it when you see employees squabble over who "owns" you as a customer:

"I saw her first!"

"I'm up next."

Is it when employees tell you to speak with someone else:

"That's not my area."

"You'll have to speak with parts to see if that's in stock."

Is it when employees ask you to be sure to ask for them:

"Be sure to ask for me. I'll write my name on this card."

What about when a person seems to be trying to optimize his or her commission by telling you pointedly when you should come back later to make the purchase:

"I'm only here Mondays and Thursday."

How does that make you feel? Are you secure, or do you feel like you are on your own and to receive good care will depend on your ability to navigate an unfamiliar terrain?

- What about *your* customers?
- What do your customers see when they interact with your firm?
- Do your employees understand their roles within cross-organizational processes, or simply within their functional organization?
- Are your employees compensated and rewarded as individuals or as team members? Is this apparent to your customers? How?
- Is knowledge a source of individual employee power and how they are valued, or is knowledge considered a company asset to be identified, harvested, and shared? How is that done? How are employees enabled to share knowledge across the business with their peers (via policies, practices, training, technology, and so on)?

- How do you both encourage and insure that your knowledge-based assets are being identified and fully levered? Is it institutionalized:

  - with formal processes to harvest valuable knowledge, company-wide, and make it available cross-functionally?

  - with measures and rewards for employees who utilize those processes?

  - with organizational enablement, such as a Chief Knowledge Officer, to provide both leadership and legitimacy to the topic?

- How are your employees paid, rewarded, and promoted? Is it based on attaining objectives linked to your paying customers and to things that customers have defined that, if performed well, would drive loyalty?

- Is performance recognition team-based, because customer-defined outcomes from your processes are the result of multi-person, cross-functional activities? And unless the team succeeds in making the customer happy, everyone fails?

- Do employees appraise one another, based on their contribution to a team effort?

- Are metrics of success not only team-based, but customer-focused and defined?

- What should you be doing differently in this regard?

- What would your key customers say you should do?

Ⓔ Ⓟ Ⓘ Ⓛ Ⓞ Ⓖ Ⓤ Ⓔ

Who Stole My Customer??

What do you think? Are the lessons learned from IBM and other major companies and the key concepts discussed in this book critical to the future success of *your* business? How far have you actually progressed beyond good managers with good intentions? What would your customers say?

- What if *you* were your customer?

- Would your firm be your preferred provider due to the implementation of customer-centered initiatives? Enterprise-wide?

- If you were the customer, what would be your ideal vision of this business? What changes might you expect to see made? How soon?

- What if your company does not change, but your competitors do? What if they implement the customer-centric concepts in this book? What might your customers do then? How easy is it for them to defect?

The question remains: In the future, will you be the one to ask, "**Who Stole My Customer??**" Or will you be the answer?

Acknowledgments

The opinions expressed in this book are the result of five years as a developer and leader of IBM's business process reengineering and governance programs and ten years as the global leader of a competency to transform clients from internally-focused, product houses to externally-focused, customer-centered enterprises.

I was privileged to meet and work with thought-leaders across the fields of research and development, academia, professional services, and executive management. It provided a unique opportunity to envision an extremely powerful set of approaches by adapting and combining what was learned from each of them.

I am extremely indebted to the following incomplete list of people:

- Jan Carlsen, an early pioneer of customer-focused (service, not product) quality at Scandinavian Airways. His Moments of Truth concept provided the perfect starting point to identify customer needs, as described to me later by Dr. N. Kano.

Acknowledgments

- Dr. Noriaki Kano, who introduced the idea of a Customer Needs hierarchy that tied to their actual behavior. His *Must-Have Quality* ideas were key inputs to the behavior-driver concepts expressed in this book as the bell-shaped curve of customer needs.

- Dr. Valerie Zeithaml, whose research to define, measure, and manage the drivers of customer satisfaction provided a methodical framework to diagnose root causes of customer dissatisfaction. Dr. Zeithaml was one of the first academic and consulting thought-leaders to shift from mere satisfaction measurement to diagnoses and prescriptive action for satisfaction *management*.

- Dr. John Henderson, whose work to align infrastructure, such as IT, with measurable business outcomes provided insights on how to take desired results for a business (such as delivering Dr. Kano's customer needs) and then reverse engineer the linkages to business infrastructure. This meshed well with Dr. Akao's techniques below.

- Dr. N. Akao, the founder of Quality Function Deployment (QFD), whose methods to weigh customer needs (such as described by Dr. Kano) and drive them into an infrastructure model (such as Dr. Henderson's) provided an element of mathematical precision to the resulting business model. This also became the basis for Cindy Adiano's automated tool to manage such complex models.

Acknowledgments

- Dr. Michael Hammer, whose pioneer concepts (and personal instruction) to break and then fundamentally redesign a business process based on desired outcomes aligned powerfully with the views of Drs. Kano, Henderson, Zeithaml, Akao, et al.

- Dr. Terry Vavra, of Marketing Metrics, Inc., whose patient counsel and books provided invaluable insights on quantitative marketing research and customer loyalty.

- Dr. William H. Davidson, who—thankfully—advised me to write books rather than articles. As I recall, he said, "A book lasts longer and becomes a thick business card." What great advice.

- Dr. James W. Cortada, the author of over 20 books, who coached my first book and then encouraged me and helped to make possible this one. Jim is selfless and a role model as a mentor.

- Timothy Moore, vice president and editor-in-chief at Prentice Hall, who brought me into the Prentice Hall publications family with his Prentice Hall Business series.

- Russell Hall, development editor at Prentice Hall, who provided invaluable assistance and made the publishing process painless.

Acknowledgments

- Vanessa Moore, production editor at Prentice Hall, whose cooperative spirit and helpfulness were invaluable and truly appreciated.

- Luis Columbus, who served as a technical reviewer and provided great encouragement.

- Finally, my thanks to you, the reader—and especially to those of you who have kindly contacted me with feedback about my books or to chat about their contents.

Thank you all!

— *Harvey Thompson*

About the Author

Harvey Thompson is an internationally recognized authority on how to grow market share by engineering a business—from the outside in—using the external customers' points of view.

As the director and managing principal for IBM Global Services, Customer Value Management Consulting, he built a worldwide network of consultants to help Fortune 500 and Global 1000 senior executives develop an actionable, *customer-defined* vision of their company as an ideal vendor—and then implement it.

As the global executive for IBM Business Innovation Services, Customer Relationship Management Consulting, his team patented *The Customer Loyalty Suite,* a set of offerings to provide clients with a customer-focused strategy, a detailed assessment, and an implementation roadmap.

His ground-breaking book, *The Customer-Centered Enterprise*, was released in 2000 by McGraw-Hill, and received immediate acclaim. Executive Book Summaries recognized it as one of the best business books of the year, and Harvard University featured and recommended it on the Harvard Business School Web site.

Other published materials include his lead article in *The Journal of Business Strategy* entitled, "What Your Customers Really Want."

Thompson has been cited as an expert on Customer Loyalty and Relationship Management and interviewed or quoted in such publications as *The Economist, Business Week, Newsweek, PC Week,* and *Investors Business Daily.* He is an editorial board member for the *Journal of Financial Services Marketing,* a keynote speaker at professional conferences, and has lectured at executive forums such as the Advanced Business Institute, in Palisades, NY, and the International Executive Education Centers in Brussels, Belgium, and Milan, Italy.

Thompson retired as an IBM executive in 2001 to pursue writing, conference speaking, client management team briefings, and private consulting. He can be reached via e-mail at *hthompson@customer-centered-ent.com*.

I·N·D·E·X

Index